Praise for
Home on the Strange

"*A delightful big-hearted book full of wit and wisdom that had me bursting into laughter every other page. Read this book no matter what stage of life you're at—it will brighten your day, and you'll see motherhood in a whole new light.*"

Amy Chua
Yale Law professor and author of *Battle Hymn of the Tiger Mother* and *Political Tribes: Group Instinct and the Fate of Nations*

"*Susan Lundy (no relation) has written a delightful and charming collection of stories about life on a small and, yes, strange, island (which I call home as well). Her warm, loving, and humorous accounts cumulatively unveil the extraordinary universal truths in the plain particulars of all our lives.*"

Derek Lundy
bestselling author of *Borderlands: Riding the Edge of America* and *The Bloody Red Hand: A Journey Through Truth, Myth, and Terror in Northern Ireland*

"*Susan Lundy takes us along with her on a rollercoaster ride through her life as a Salt Spring Islander, a wife, a mother, a journalist, and a keen observer on the foibles and challenges of living a contemporary west coast life. She writes with humour, honesty, and humanity. And hope. Her book is something we all need right now.*"

Ian Haysom
bestselling author of *Grandfathered: Dispatches from the Trenches of Modern Grandparenthood*

D1488065

the Strange

Chronicles of Motherhood,

Mayhem, and Matters of the Heart

Susan J. Lundy

HERITAGE

Heritage House Publishing Company Ltd.
heritagehouse.ca

Cataloguing information available from Library and Archives Canada

978-1-77203-364-9 (pbk)
978-1-77203-365-6 (ebook)

Edited by Paula Marchese
Proofread by Nandini Thaker
Cover and interior book design by Jacqui Thomas
Cover images: Cultura Creative RF / Alamy Stock photo (*front*);
Creative Market by Anugraha Design (bricks, *back*)

The interior of this book was produced on 100% post-consumer recycled
paper, processed chlorine free, and printed with vegetable-based inks.

Heritage House gratefully acknowledges that the land on which we live
and work is within the traditional territories of the Lkwungen (Esquimalt
and Songhees), Malahat, Pacheedaht, Scia'new, T'Sou-ke, and W̱SÁNEĆ
(Pauquachin, Tsartlip, Tsawout, Tseycum) Peoples.

We acknowledge the financial support of the Government of Canada through
the Canada Book Fund (CBF) and the Canada Council for the Arts, and
the Province of British Columbia through the British Columbia Arts Council
and the Book Publishing Tax Credit.

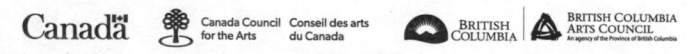

25 24 23 22 21 1 2 3 4 5

Printed in Canada

For Danica, Sierra,
and all the men and women
who grace this book.

←

Contents

Author's Note

←

Throughout the last three decades of working in the media, I've written many columns, first for the *Gulf Islands Driftwood*, then for Black Press Media, and finally for *Boulevard* magazine. Although I didn't realize it at the time, the columns became perfect conduits for memories. So many anecdotes would have been lost had I not faced all those deadlines. In the following pages are many of these columns, written, rewritten, and honed over the years. I hope you enjoy reading them.

Prologue:
In the Beginning

←

When it comes to motherhood, my mother and I were more than a generation apart. Worlds separated us on the issue of domesticity. Her house gleamed; mine had a dull glint. The smell of fresh baking wafted through her front door and down the driveway, while the scent of wet dog lingered in my home. The closest my kids got to warm apple pie was finding a Spartan in their lunch boxes. She ironed. My daughter was three before she saw an iron and wondered what the heck Mommy was doing with it.

On the other hand, my mother and I are like other mothers the world over because motherhood connects us all.

How did I get here? I wondered sometimes, a decade into parenting. How did this career-pining, quasi academic get to the place where a sentimental TV commercial could turn her heart to mush? How did I land in this world where children were more miraculous than an A from Professor Valgardson or a raise in my paycheque? For my mother, the path was more obvious: school, nurse's training, then marriage and kids with career left behind. For me, born in the '60s and fed on feminism in the '70s and '80s, the choice was less clear. Modern women did not have to stay home, wash the walls, and bake three pies every week. Clipping coupons was out. Dress suits were in. I could motor out of the driveway in the morning, delve into engrossing and stimulating work (setting my own hours), bring home a fat cheque, put my feet up, and read the newspaper. (I seemed to forget that Mom wouldn't be around to cook dinner and clean the cobwebs.)

"Family" never sat big on my agenda, dwarfed as it was by "career" and the hope of writing my way to fame or fortune. Journalism came along a little later, but it fit the vision. During my fourth year in the creative writing department at the University of Victoria, I took a summer co-op job as a reporter at the *Gulf Islands Driftwood* newspaper on Salt Spring Island, just a ferry ride away from Victoria, where I grew up. I saw it as a stepping stone to much bigger, more lucrative opportunities in the future.

But then I met and interviewed a local stonemason/carver/photographer named Derrick. We immediately connected and moved in together three weeks later. So Salt Spring became home. I commuted to Victoria to finish my degree and took on a permanent role at the *Driftwood*. My career continued to loom large until my two daughters came along. Then I looked into their eyes and—although I kept working at the newspaper for the next few decades—thoughts or desires for a glamorous career diminished and remained distant until both girls had graduated high school. Nothing mattered more than family.

Once firmly entrenched in the mother-of-babies phase, I gobbled up books and spent hours on the phone with other new—formerly intellectual, now mushy-brained—mothers. We analyzed everything. We scrutinized each of our children's stages, thumbing through books for advice and comparisons, and agonizing over apparent differences. We wondered how our own mothers managed to produce such wonderful women with nothing more than Dr. Spock. Then we discovered that we weren't always wonderful, that our parenting skills faltered at times. Then we felt guilty. And we analyzed all that, too.

As I look back on years of being a mom, it is the overwhelming passion for my family that overrides everything.

I'm sure my own mother felt the same.

PART ONE

Family First

Motherhood

← THE CRANBERRY →

Back in 1986, I was twenty-one and still at university when I moved with my boyfriend Derrick into the first home I could sort of call my own. The rental house, named The Cranberry, had recently been vacated by the boyfriend's ex-wife. It came with furniture, a pair of stepkids, and a gerbil.

Built in the early 1900s, and supposedly haunted by the ghost of gin-drinking Mary Brown, The Cranberry sat on seventy-five acres of rolling Salt Spring Island grassland and had its own private lake. Bright and cozy on the inside, with a sun-soaked deck out back and a spectacular view that changed colours with the seasons, The Cranberry was a slice of heaven most days.

But it definitely came with challenges. Insulation (grass) between the logs had long since disappeared, and the building sagged in the corners. The floors peaked at the seam between the living room and the kitchen and then sloped away in opposite directions.

And the very ex-wife-ness of this house was a bit daunting, especially in the kitchen, where tall baby-blue cupboards housed shelves of homemade preserves and jars of beans and spices and other dried goods. The decade that separated the ex-wife and me in age thrust us into different eras. When I was eating Campbell's soup in my mother's 1970s kitchen, Derrick's ex was living off the land, digging up rutabagas from the garden, soaking pinto beans overnight, and bubbling up dinner in a slow-cooking pot. While she was doing Lamaze, cloth-diapering babies, sewing, baking, canning, and scrubbing the corners of her kitchen with bristle brushes, I was studying creative writing at university. I found those jars of preserves more intimidating than an essay on Margaret Atwood.

During the years at The Cranberry, our little family expanded as we took in a stray cat—who immediately pro-duced kittens—and a big dozy dog. But there were other creatures, too. Here, March didn't come in like a lamb or a lion. It came in like a frog. One night the moon appeared as usual in the silent, still air. The next night there'd be one or two tentative croaks. But by the end of the week, the newly awakened amphibians roared like an assembly of sci-fi spaceships, revving their engines and preparing for flight. The sound overpowered everything. The frogs fired up at dusk and bellowed like bagpipes throughout most of the night.

Other wildlife found its way into our house, like the extended mice families, the spider named Fred in the bath-room, the occasional bat, and a hornets' nest in the attic. I didn't find the mice too troublesome—as long as they stayed in the walls. The spider Fred wove his silky webs and kept the area free of bugs. It was the hornets, which inevitably found their way from the attic through the doors, walls, or ceiling into our bedroom, that we refused to accept as room-mates, devising several methods to expedite their demise. (When all else fails, use a vacuum cleaner!)

But it wasn't the creatures that finally prompted us to move. Salt Spring Island enjoys a fairly temperate, west coast climate, but there were a few winter nights during our years at The Cranberry that forced us to adopt drastic keep-warm measures. We'd drape blankets over windows and entranceways and live by the wood stove. But one winter the temperature plummeted and we awoke to find our bedside drinking water frozen. Downstairs, we had no running water at all because the pipes had burst. And in the bathroom the water in the toilet bowl had frozen as solid as a skating rink. Within a year, we'd bought a house that didn't have the word "rustic" in its description, and moved into a warmer, less-critter-filled abode.

The move from The Cranberry in August 1991 precipitated many more firsts in my life: first mortgage, the birth of my first daughter (just three weeks later) . . . and, eventually, our first bathroom door that locked! But The Cranberry, which sadly burned down a few years ago, will always have a place in my heart as the first house I could sort of call my own.

← HOME ON THE STRANGE →

Family life began for me on Halloween night, 1986.

That's the night Derrick's ex-wife and her partner moved out and I—with the boyfriend of five months—moved in. The house at The Cranberry came with a pair of kids: a boy, aged eight (hostile), and girl, eleven (moderately friendly).

The move afforded a reuniting of the children with their father's gerbil—a selling point of my relationship with him. I knew I could love a man with a gerbil, especially one called Quasimodo.

"Don't touch the gerbil," Derrick warned his son not five minutes after we arrived and the ex left. "It bites."

"It won't bite me," said Dylan.

"Don't touch the gerbil," Dad repeated. Jessica moved over by the cage, echoing the order in a stern elder-sibling voice.

Dylan, of course, reached into the cage to stroke the warm and furry Quasimodo, who, startled from slumber, sunk its sharp teeth into Dylan's finger.

Dylan shrieked. "It bit me! You—you ... asshole!"

"Dad!" Jessica shouted. "Dylan swore! And he touched the gerbil!"

I—twenty-one and unused to children at all—watched the unfolding scene with quiet horror. The new boyfriend suddenly had more baggage. Like kids with sibling rivalry. And, apparently, children who did not respond with soldier-like acquiescence to direct orders.

That night the children dressed for Halloween in costumes that turned out to be rather appropriate to their personalities— Jessica as a sparkling gypsy, Dylan as Count Dracula. Dylan insisted on plastering his face with makeup, paying special attention to the red drips of "blood" drooling from his mouth, which, by the time we left for trick-or-treating, had smeared into blush-like rivers on the sides of his face.

I had my new family.

Step-parenting was tough, but, luckily for me, I had my own "baby" in those years. Dexter came to us in year two of our life at The Cranberry. He was not a bright dog, but he was definitely my dog, chewing everything that belonged to the man of the house. Derrick's socks were the first to go. Then his beloved saddlebags, the wires that connected his stereo, and finally, the stereo itself. I merely lost a bathrobe.

From the start, Dexter exhibited superiority over everything and anything feline. Cats belonged up trees, and kittens were on the earth merely as live, wriggling rawhide. He and Shishwa, the stray cat who had arrived on the scene before him, developed a mutual disdain and basically ignored each other. But her kittens were another matter, and when she birthed a second litter just six weeks prior to being hit and killed by a car, we had to keep dog and kittens separate.

However, one kitten, Alf, could not bear to be away from Dexter, whom he immediately adopted as Dad. Dexter responded by carrying the kitten—head neatly inserted between his jaws—to the lawn, where he pretended Alf was one of Derrick's socks. Alf loved it. Dexter tried to run him up a tree. Alf slept on his head and nibbled affectionately on his ear. Alf refused to eat cat food and, eventually, it became common to see them standing side-by-side eating from the same bowl.

While Dexter endured his time with Alf, he waged a personal war with the racoons that roamed the property of our second home at night. Even in his old age, when he'd mostly lie by the door, stiff with arthritis, the sound of a raccoon could propel him back to his youth. He'd shoot from the doorway like a bullet to chase them, aches and pains forgotten.

One night, I was in the dining room, sitting by the door that led to the porch while Dexter snoozed peacefully beside me. A raccoon family sidled onto the deck to nibble on dog food left in a bowl by the door. Suddenly, Dexter realized that the enemy was chowing down on his Sunday dinner. With an angry yelp, he dove toward the offending animals, attempting to dive right through the cat door. Unfortunately, only his head could fit through it, and he hung there, barking and sputtering while the raccoons darted away.

Dexter, my "son," turned into Dexter, "a dog," when my first daughter was born. I remember apologizing to him in advance as I left for the hospital. Later, a fellow mother and I commiserated about the lowly spot our dogs had taken next to our children. Their main role in life was to provide advance warning if someone was walking up to the door when we were still in our pajamas. On family walks they became cougar decoys.

But having him put down was tough, even though the time had come. I was shocked by the force of grief that struck and then stayed with me for days. Thirteen years is a long time, and Dexter spanned two parts of my life—the five years at The Cranberry and all those years marked by the various stages of step-parenting and then parenthood at our second house.

A mom never forgets her first born.

← THE AWAKENING →

The first inkling that I might want to become pregnant occurred one night as Gail, my friend and co-worker at the *Driftwood*, and I drank beer in Moby's Pub on Salt Spring Island. As we stared into the future, we saw ourselves as mothers. Not our mothers, of course. We would never discuss the pros and cons of various diapers. We would never disappear into the world of playgrounds and baby clothing and Lego and vomiting children. We would never, ever wear stretchy pants with elastic waistbands or drive automatic vehicles.

This could work! I went home to woo my new husband with the idea.

When the "you are pregnant!" call came from the doctor (pre-home-pregnancy-test years), I took the first step any student of new life would take. I purchased the book *What to Expect When You're Expecting* the first time around and *Siblings Without Rivalry* the second time.

After speaking with the doctor, Derrick and I immediately and wisely decided to tell no one until the three-month potential miscarriage period had passed. But five minutes later, I phoned my mother. And Gail. And then Derrick called his parents. And his brothers. And soon the whole island knew, so it was no surprise when I went and bought the tell-tale book the next morning.

I grew and grew that spring and summer, but my wardrobe shrank. Eventually, I settled into one pair of white polyester pants that expanded with me through the spring and summer and ultimately became a mass of limp, thread-strained material that waited in a defeated pile on the floor each night until called upon for action the next day. I bought one white maternity dress, into which I simply could not believe I'd ever fit. And then I grew out of it.

While I could sadly survey my sorry wardrobe in one glance, clothes for the kicking and squirming unborn were amassing. My mother, expecting her first grandchild, had set her idle-for-two-decades sewing machine into action. She purchased new knitting needles that flew through the air at remarkable speeds, and heave-hoed me through wool shops and knitting departments, and set me gazing upon pattern magazines. (Little could any of us know then, but the unborn, who popped out small enough, would grow into a butterball at such remarkable speed that the resulting little red jacket fit for approximately two days.) Boxes of baby clothing and foreign-looking items with lots of straps arrived from previously unknown people, and I found myself waddling into baby garb stores at a surprising rate.

And the book consumption turned into a feast. I read everything on pregnancy and birth, keeping notes, following the baby's development. I took to singing "You've Got a Friend" in the bathtub and the car. I threw in a few other tunes—some Beatles and Stones for good taste—but stuck with the James Taylor song in the hopes that it would someday soothe my baby's colicky stomach by subliminally sending her back to the comfort of the womb.

Cocooned in the world of pregnancy, I read absolutely nothing on the postnatal period. I wasn't interested in diapers or diets or baby growth charts. But I could tell you exactly what would happen from the moment the first labour pain gripped my uterus. It would hurt (but how bad could it be, really?), and it would take about three hours (my mom's labours lasted between ninety minutes and three hours), and right afterward, I'd have a flat stomach again.

A day or two after my maternity leave from the *Driftwood* started, I found myself restless and back at the office. And it was here that, two weeks before my due date, my water broke. Hours later, I was easily managing the contractions (told you!) when a more serious one hit. Suddenly panicked and thinking the baby was going arrive any minute, I grabbed my somewhat nonchalant, done-this-before husband, and we headed to the hospital. The nurses were cucumber-cool and unruffled; they seemed to have no idea my body was being ripped in half. As it turned out, I was only one centimetre dilated. Nine centimetres to go! This was not fun. For the next several hours I wandered about the hospital in my huge yellow robe, moaning through contractions while Derrick snored peacefully in my hospital bed.

It took eighteen hours to birth Danica. Lying on my back in the hospital bed after leaving the delivery room, I put my hand on my stomach. Yes! So flat, where just hours ago sat a mountain. Then I rolled onto my side and this great mass of stomach sort of spilled over onto the bed beside me. I paused for a moment, and then I shrugged.

I looked into my baby's eyes and thought, *Oh well, I can wear stretchy pants.*

← PINK ALL OVER →

I'm grateful social media didn't exist in the baby years. I'd have been beyond obnoxious: here's a photo of Danica looking at a tree; here's a photo of Sierra sitting in a chair; here's a photo of the girls smiling—it's a bit blurry, but can you see the new tooth popping out of Sierra's gums?

In those years, little existed beyond babies. I recall arriving at my parents' home one morning with a cooing baby Danica. We walked into the bathroom, and there I was in the mirror. But it wasn't me. I'd slept the night before with wet hair, and now it had sprung out in all directions like a furry Russian hat. My eyes were puffy and a spot of dried coffee sat in the corner of my mouth. Danica, on the other hand, was bright and clean, with combed curly locks and laces neatly tied on her shiny white shoes.

Danica was nicely dressed in those days, but not in the way I had envisioned. I assumed that since I liked denim, I'd dress her in little denim pants and little jean shirts and jackets. Anything else would be yellow, green, or blue. At all costs, I would avoid pink, and I would never, ever purchase a frilly dress.

Then, as I wheeled Danica down a bumpy road in a stroller one day, someone asked the heart-ripping question: "How old is he?" He! So out came the pink sleepers. Out came the barrettes; out came the frills. At Danica's first Easter she was six months old. We gathered at my parents' house for a special dinner, and she emerged more dressed than the turkey. I stuffed her into a mass of pink frills and lace, heaved her legs into white tights, and stuck little black patent shoes on her feet. Worst of all, my mother took photographs of everyone's favourite cherub, so she will exist forever in pink.

But in fact, life became pink all over. My friend Sandy and I took to walking through town, pushing our offspring in strollers, talking about nothing that didn't relate to babies. The sun warmed our faces. Pink blossoms poked from trees in the park; even the sound of cars motoring by became a happy hum in the background. Life was still and gentle and . . . pink.

One day we joined other new parents in a coffee shop, and, for a split second, I emerged from baby bliss long enough to notice our strange antics. We made weird faces and noises. We gurgled, burped, blew bubbles, and sang unlikely little songs. We performed face gymnastics and body contortions—anything to elicit a beatific baby smile.

One of the burly, masculine men at our table said, "Try this."

He leaned toward Danica and started clucking. Soon we were all clucking. Then Danica swatted at my friend Sandy, and I murmured, "You're supposed to honk when she touches your nose."

So Sandy honked. Then we all honked.

A few decades later, the world around me and my kids is a little bigger, and things aren't so pink. But I've discovered that your babies never really stop being the centre of your universe. Just check my social media pages.

As September rolls around each year, and kids everywhere start shuffling out of the summer nest back to school, I'm struck again by the ongoing role that "letting go" plays in parenting.

By the time our children actually leave home, we've spent the previous decades slowly relinquishing ties—dropping them off at the first day of kindergarten; then years later, lying awake, watching the clock *tick, tick, tick* toward curfew, and, still later, sending them off on a plane to Thailand.

I easily recall the first day I returned to work as a mom. There I sat, car idling, unwilling to press my foot to the gas pedal. In the rear-view mirror, I could see little Danica, wearing a bright red sweater, sitting on Daddy's shoulders, and waving goodbye. I sobbed the entire way to work. I arrived and rushed into my office dungeon, and immediately called home. Guessing it was me, Derrick didn't answer. So I let my fretting voice blare across the (pre-voicemail) answering machine.

"How is she?" I demanded. "Put her on the phone."

No answer. So I began singing a soothing lullaby. That got him, and he picked up.

"She's just fine," he announced. "In fact, she began crawling five minutes after you left, took her first step about three minutes later, and now we're reading Tolstoy."

"Very funny." I hung up and called again thirty minutes later. And thirty minutes after that. I went home at lunchtime.

But as time marched on, we needed daycare, and I dreaded it. It was bad enough that I had to trudge off to work and leave my precious gem in the care of Dad or Nana. (I mean, really, did my mom have enough experience? Would she know what to do?) But to hand my child over to a stranger? Expose her to the worldliness of other children? My friend Sandy—who didn't need to work and spent a lot of time reading parenting literature—helpfully suggested that placing children in daycare was, in essence, putting them on the path to juvenile crime. I expressed the opinion that a little socialization was probably a good thing . . . but I couldn't help picturing my daughter behind bars.

So one September afternoon, with great angst rolling in my stomach, nine-month-old Danica and I approached a little white building that housed a neighbourhood daycare. My glum mood lifted a few notches at the sight of the multicoloured climbing apparatus, swings, slides, and tricycles. We stepped up to the door, knocked, and entered the threshold of a whole new era.

Danica pulled herself up on a couch and stood, surveying the room while I sniffled a bit. Then it happened. Little Rosalie, just a few months older than Danica, toddled over, put her arms around Danica, and hugged her. It was a sign! The next day, I dropped her off for a few hours while I worked. I picked up a happy child, who did not appear any closer to delinquency.

In the end, both my daughters spent happy days in daycare, even forging some life-long friendships. And aside from incurring a few traffic tickets, I'm happy to report that neither child has been carried off in a police car or yet spent any time behind bars.

← KNOCKED UP . . . AGAIN →

I was a pro the second time I became pregnant. I knew the bookstore was the first stop, and the next stop had to be a candlelit restaurant. A nice romantic dinner, just the two of us.

"What?" I asked my husband. "You haven't seen me for the last year? I'm lost in a sea of babies and diapers and fellow mothers? Ah, and you're feeling a little left out . . . Well, remember how just about a month ago, we sort of discussed the fact that Danica was turning one, and maybe it was time to start thinking . . . at least acknowledging, somewhere in the universe, that maybe we'd want to do it again? And you said, you'd like to practise, anyway. And so we practised? And last time it took months and months. And well . . . ah, this time it took two weeks! And you are going to be a father! Again!"

When I announced my pregnancy to Sandy, she brought out a book with footnotes whose author recommended the importance of spacing your children by precisely three years. She was pretty grave about the whole thing.

I worked hard to prepare Danica for the new baby. One book suggested offering up a special gift to number one the day you bring number two home. So I found a beautiful old wooden rocking horse that I bought, sanded down, and, over a period of months, while Danica napped, painted white with a glittering gold mane and hooves. As my stomach grew rotund, we would lie together at night singing "Kumbaya" and "Hush, Little Baby" (which became Sierra's song as much as "You've Got a Friend" was Danica's), and she would stick her little hands and lips on my moving belly and say "Goodnight, baby."

So I knew she was fully prepared to have a sibling, would love her unconditionally, help with the diapers, and would remain calm when baby number two cried and needed attention.

Being a "birth pro" the second time around, I left the getting to the hospital part of it a bit late. The typically ten-minute drive was punctuated by my contractions that forced Derrick to pull the car over and wait while I breathed through them—once even as a couple of teenage girls wandered by. Also, because of my frantic, last-minute call to "Go now!" Derrick happened to be barefoot. For some reason, he thought we could stop at the drugstore and pick up some flip-flops (while I heaved and writhed in the parking lot). I screamed something incoherent and that ended that idea.

Forty-five minutes after arriving at the hospital, Sierra was born. Danica, just a month short of two at the time, was there in the care of my mom. She took one look at Sierra on the delivery table and said, "Mine. My baby."

Today, I'm glad I had the girls close together despite the warnings from Sandy's book. (She did space her first two three years apart.) As the girls grew, their developmental stages weren't that far off from each other, and over the years, they developed an intense friendship.

Sierra's personality gradually emerged over the next six months. She was a gentler soul than her spirited sister who nevertheless benefitted from having a somewhat autocratic (my thesaurus gives this as a synonym for "bossy") sibling, learning to assert herself as the years passed. The future looked bright—especially since I was now a pro at this parenting thing.

← IN THE ICU →

The dreamy days of babies and small children changed dramatically when Sierra became ill at six months old and we spent several days in the Pediatric Intensive Care Unit at BC Children's Hospital in Vancouver. There, everything was reduced to a heartbeat, and only the lives of those children who were patients mattered.

Sierra's hospital story actually began with Danica, who snored almost from birth and had periods of sleep apnea, where she would stop breathing as she slept and then suddenly gasp for air. This continued throughout the early part of her sleep and sometimes into the late hours of the night. I finally took her to an ear, nose, and throat (ENT) specialist, who said, rather disdainfully, that I should help Danica blow her nose four times a day. I left his office feeling silly to have been worried.

Then Sierra came along, and her apnea was even worse. I would lie beside her, listen to her breathe in and out, and then wait. Sometimes her gasp for air took too long, and I'd give her a little jolt.

Awake, Sierra was as happy and playful as any six-month-old, so it was difficult for anyone, myself included, to consider her as "sick." I took Sierra to a naturopathic physician, who prescribed homeopathic pills to open her air passages—they didn't work— and finally convinced my GP to book an "urgent" appointment with a specialist. But even that was three weeks away.

By this time Sierra was waking with each bout of apnea, giving a short wail, and then falling back to sleep. Derrick and I sat in the living room after putting the girls to bed and listened with distress as cries followed by silence punctuated the air. Finally, her apnea became so acute that we sat holding her upright all night, trying to find a position to help her breathe. The next day, I took her to emergency at the local hospital, where she gurgled and crawled happily across the crisp white sheets. I still felt apologetic as I explained the situation. The doctor was not overly concerned, but he decided to send us across the water to Victoria General Hospital.

Sierra, buckled into her car seat behind me, tried to doze off as we drove along the highway but kept being awakened— even as she sat upright—by the apnea. Fear suddenly and finally gripped me.

"Hold on," I told her. "We're almost there."

At Victoria General, she was booked into the ICU for observation and connected to heart, oxygen, and breathing monitors. I was sent to a breast pump and a little sleeping room, only to be awakened at 4:30 AM by an alarmed nurse, who said they'd discovered that each time Sierra stopped breathing, her heart rate dropped dangerously low. They planned an immediate emergency operation to insert a short breathing tube through her nose.

A series of X-rays—for which she was plastered up against a wall, limbs splayed—followed, but the ENTs could find few abnormalities other than extremely large, but not inflamed, tonsils. They decided to insert a longer breathing tube, hook her up to morphine, and send her via helicopter to BC Children's Hospital. There was no room for me on the eleven-passenger helicopter because the doctor brought along nurses and an intern, and so I was forced to take a ferry to Vancouver. My family rallied around us, with Mom going off to Salt Spring to help Derrick with Danica and my dad driving me through sheets of rain to Vancouver. BC Children's Hospital greeted me with a big cheery "mouse tree" activity centre and colourful facades over the elevators. It felt comfortably child-centred and somehow soothing. This was fortunate because I had become a bit unhinged by this point.

All physicians at Children's must be pediatricians before they specialize into specific areas of medicine. This makes them great in their dealing with kids and their parents. Sierra's new ENT considered her X-rays and symptoms, eliminated the possibility of a chest infection or pertussis, and decided to perform an emergency operation to remove her tonsils and adenoids. He diagnosed her with obstructive sleep apnea and believed that as she fell asleep, her tongue relaxed against her large tonsils, blocking off the airway. She would be the second youngest child to ever have this operation at BC Children's Hospital.

Waiting is a big part of life in the ICU, and I spent hours in the parents' lounge, sitting on one of the couches, trying to read, writing occasionally, but mostly just watching. Exhaustion weighed on my body like a living presence. I existed between the lounge, the cafeteria, and my sleeping room at Ronald McDonald House, down the road from the hospital.

Inside the ICU, parents clung to tiny hands that were barely visible under splints and bandages. The children lay in a tangle of wires and tape, surrounded by monitors, flashing screens, and clusters of doctors and nurses. The air hummed with a certain hushed calm, but the sight of all these tiny bodies lying prone belied any sense of peace.

I slipped into a world that revolved around the ICU— standing at Sierra's bedside, waiting in the parents' lounge during the five non-visiting hours each day, walking the bleak trek to the cafeteria, and sitting at a breast pump in the mothers' room. Some parents shared their experiences; others couldn't speak. But everyone held a look of anguish and intensity—so different from the people with children in regular wards—that spoke louder than words.

Although Sierra was young to be undergoing an adenotonsillectomy, and although I was devastated, I knew it was unlikely she'd die. But for many in the ICU, each day of life is a gift.

In a small bed by Sierra's slept a nine-week-old baby who was born with a faulty trachea. The baby's mother, Linda, and I spoke quietly in the mothers' room, and I learned that if the baby survived the night, she would undergo an operation to cut open her trachea and sew it up with a piece of skin from her heart.

The baby did make it through the night, and the next day Linda and her husband rigidly waited out the three-hour operation. When the baby returned to the ICU, their faces were washed in joy and relief. The baby's heart continued to beat through the day and night; however, it would be days before doctors could safely predict her future. But for now, on the mothers' room sign-in sheet, Linda wrote, "Today is a wonderful day!"

I saw Linda and her baby packing up to go home two weeks later as I returned to BC Children's Hospital, this time with Danica, who would undergo the same operation as her sister. Linda and I hugged, and she seemed lighter, like her anguish had fallen away.

Today, my stomach still tightens when I realize how critical Sierra's condition was; in fact, I've read literature since that considers there to be a link between obstructive sleep apnea and sudden infant death syndrome. But I'll never forget my experience in the ICU, and I'll never forget Linda. Because each day we have with our children is a gift—"a wonderful day."

Mayhem

The parenting books eagerly lauded the advantages of breast-feeding babies—for years, in fact—but were less precise when it came to the weaning side of things other than stating, "Don't worry, be happy, and it will happen."

One spring there were three of us mothers—me, Gail, and another friend, also named Sandy—who were becoming increasingly horrified as, one after another, our children's third birthdays passed. Still guzzling away, these kids now had the skills to request (read whine, be coy, or demand) a breast milk snack and unzip, unbutton, and forcibly dive for their target. Gail's daughter, Chloe, who began reading just before she turned three, was able to spell "breast," look up the word in her *Charlie Brown Dictionary*, and read out the definition.

We staged several months of worried conversations. We'd all read a book about nursing toddlers, which blithely noted all the advantages of nursing children past infancy but had little to say about weaning. I spoke with other normal-looking mothers who readily admitted breastfeeding their children to age four and even older.

Sandy called to say her daughter had stood up on a chair at the dinner table in front of guests the night before and openly debated which breast—Sandy's right or left —she loved more and which she would attack first following the meal. Sierra happily told me she would never give up her "tiddy," and, if it dried up, I could just take a few swigs from a milk carton and solve that problem.

It was all very well for the World Health Organization to recommend nursing children until their second birthday or later. But as it became more and more important in their lives, we wondered, how did you take it away?

"Well, I think I'm ready to write something about nursing," I told Sandy a year or so later. After all, one by one, we had somehow managed to remove our Very Large Children from our breasts.

"Remember how we worried about it?" I laughed disparagingly at my former self. "Thought it would never end? Moaned for hours about it on the phone?"

And here we were now, another stage well behind us, breezily debating schooling techniques and not thinking once about nursing preschoolers. And really, it was all so simple.

"How did we do it anyway?" I asked.

"Well," Sandy said, her voice dropping. "We, ah, bribed them."

"Oh yeah." I fell silent.

"And we . . . well . . . we gave them bottles."

"Oh yeah."

Great. We weaned our four-year-olds to bottles. What kind of example is that? I suddenly recalled the night I said to Sierra, "Listen, if you can go ten whole days without nursing, I'll buy you a big girl present."

The power of consumerism worked. The nursing ended; we bought a new doll. But I did catch her frowning darkly at me periodically, perhaps aware that she'd been duped.

In the end, it turned out that mothers of nursing pre-schoolers have one advantage—the ability to negotiate (bribe). But when you're in the fog of it, mothering a child who apparently loves you mostly for your mammary glands, weaning may appear a formidable, near-impossible task. So here are words of lofty wisdom: Don't worry, be happy, and it will happen.

← PLAYTIME →

Sometimes, when my kids were preschoolers, I tossed aside the Lego, the one hundred-piece puzzles, the games of "let's pre-tend I'm a cute fluffy kitty, and you, Momma, are a ferocious, two-headed alien," and found something really useful to play with my daughters, who were by then curly-haired blondes with willpower and endless energy. I created two games, one for periods of exhaustion; the other to coincide with rare bursts of energy.

"Let's play naturopathic physician," I'd suggest, giving a modern spin to the old favourite as I eyed the couch and pic-tured myself prone.

Then I'd plop down on its cushiony surface and attempt to doze off while the girls used a mixture of shamanism, medi-eval doctoring equipment, and ancient crystal techniques to cure me of whatever ailment (usually death) had overtaken me on this day. They opened my mouth to check my heart. They placed a badminton racket on my face. They used lotion (after I removed the jar of vapor rub) to coat my feet.

Often they'd chant little healing verses while I slipped off into another world, only to emerge refreshed and to find my now-bored physicians happily arguing about whose turn it was to be the princess and who must be the dreaded prince.

However, as good as this game was in theory, it didn't always weave its intended path; there were dangers, such as the "healing the hair" activity. In this process, a razor-edged club, disguised as a brush, was banged into the scalp and ripped down the length of the hair. From the carnage, there emerged several thoroughly knotted shapes called "braids" by the physicians-turned-hairstylists.

Once, as I relaxed into the couch and let my eyes get a little heavy, I was jolted awake by a sharp pain in my arm. Four big, innocent eyes stared at me as I looked at the ink mark. "You needed a shot, Momma."

I also endured teeth cleaning, suffocation, and nasty comments about stubble growing on my calves. But, honestly, it was a useful game.

I drummed up the second activity in one of those curious moments when I felt inspired to clean the fridge and vacuum the big wooden beams in the living room. I adopted a French accent, called myself Marie, and explained that I was the royal maid of the royal princesses here to clean the royal palace. I actually had some success at cleaning the house before I was diverted into preparing royal snacks, defleaing the royal hound, and mopping up a royal food mess.

Toys and games aside, I loved watching the pure and sweet imagination that goes into child's play. Most often, the girls would flitter in the room and about me as I washed dishes and prepared endless snacks, and I caught only sparks of their conversations. But once in a while, I'd hear them chattering in the back seat of the car, like the time I picked up one of Sierra's friends for a play date. The two immediately launched into their latest game.

"Let's pretend we're princesses with horses."

"A black horse and a white horse."

"All the horses in the world."

"And a unicorn."

"All the unicorns in the world!"

"And we didn't have any parents."

"Just sisters."

"All the sisters in the world!"

Later, as I watched the two create a wonderland of very deliberately placed books and blankets and dolls, I suggested that perhaps I should play with the Barbies while they put away the groceries.

The young visitor fixed me with a stern look.

"We are the children. You are the adult," she said. "We get to play, and you have to clean the house."

← PARENTING PURRLA →

The parenting books said it was fine—all good in fact!—for children to attach themselves to toys, blankets, or any other "transitional objects." Apparently, 70 percent of children develop these strong attachments, but the literature doesn't offer much advice on replacing these items should something horrific happen.

So when Danica glued herself to a kitten stuffie called Purrla, my mother anxiety moved beyond ensuring the safety of my kids to constant consideration of the whereabouts and good health of a stuffed cat.

Cozily tucked under an arm, the purring (rattling) Purrla travelled everywhere with Danica, starting from the moment it (she) appeared under the Christmas tree in Danica's kindergarten year. Soccer with a stuffie? No problem, Purrla clung to an armpit. School play with a stuffie? No problem, Purrla dressed in a miniature version of Danica's costume and went on stage, too.

"She is not stuffed," Danica claimed. "She is filled with my love."

More than once in the darkness of night, a blood-freezing scream from Danica's room pierced my peaceful slumber and sent me stumbling to her side.

"Purrla!" Danica would groggily groan.

I'd pluck Purrla from the floor, deposit her back in the bed, and take several deep breaths to calm my hammering heart.

I suffered recurring nightmares centred on issues of loss, specifically the loss of Purrla. What if she *fell overboard on a ferry*? What if she *tumbled into an outhouse hole*? The terror of it could grip me at any time—like the day an American tourist strolled by.

"My daughter used to have one of those," he drawled, pointing at Purrla (at which point Danica tucked her pet into her shirt and deliberately turned her back). "Called her Yellow Dog. Got so thur was only one ear left. Carried that ear everywhere."

He added ominously, "Better git yurself another one. Just in case."

His family life was apparently saved by the friend of a friend of a friend who just happened to find an exact Yellow Dog replica "in Nurth Carolina of all places." Dear God. I'd ordered Purrla from a time-limited, only-available-here offer at least a year earlier. Replacement would be tricky.

I wasn't the only one suffering Purrla nightmares. Danica's kindergarten teacher, Frances, experienced a few of her own. Purrla became a member of her class, having her own turn whacking the piñata, and inspiring a full-school hunt on the day she was misplaced and eventually found "hiding" under a table.

"Just like kittens will do!" said a relieved Danica.

Fellow kindergarteners fell into a horrified hush when, as another child held Purrla, one of her whiskers got caught, pulling from one side of her face to the other. Danica gave a hysterical, my-baby-is-fatally-wounded scream, and a grim silence fell over the classroom. Frances dug out a needle and managed to fix the offending whisker.

It was tense, she confided later, still a little pale from the experience.

Purrla stuck like glue to Danica's underarm for the next eighteen months. She became ratty, with balled-up fur—but Danica's attachment was unyielding. And because Purrla became an appendage, Danica never lost her. Purrla was just always there, tucked under her arm.

Then, on the first day of Grade 2, Danica looked mournfully at her bedraggled pet and decided that, in the best interest of Purrla's health, the kitty should stay home and rest on her pillow. Danica continued to sleep with her pet (rattle, rattle all night long) and did not start leaving her behind when we travelled until five years later.

Slowly my fear of loss subsided . . . but even these days, before Danica arrives home for the holidays, I scoot up to her room, breathing through a little tremble of fear, to make sure Purrla is still there, waiting on Danica's pillow.

← DRIVING QUESTIONS →

Recently I met a dad, who, as the father of an eight- and a ten-year-old, seemed stunned to discover that his life's work now involved taxiing children around. I smiled empathetically, patted his arm, and said, "It will get worse."

But as I look back over the eighteen or so years I spent driving my kids here, there, and everywhere, I know for a fact: It was a blessing. We had the best times in the car, sang the most songs, had the deepest conversations.

I can also see that, as the years went by, the nature of driving kids around changed, from those very early days when they could suddenly read every road sign we'd pass—and did—to years later, when I'd pick up a carload of post-party teens at 2 AM, no questions asked.

But amidst those early car-bound years sits that unforgettable stage: the Question Period, when queries weren't asked, they were sprayed at you like a pellet gun. Danica was six and Sierra four, when I decided to count the number of questions I faced during one hour in the car. Danica fired up the minute tires touched the pavement, asking a total of fifty-four questions. Sierra, who had to wait for those infrequent occasions when Danica paused to catch her breath, managed to squeeze in eight, for an approximate total of one question per minute. No wonder my brain throbbed.

Later, in studying their questions, I discovered they fell into several categories. For example, there were the layered questions that grew like a tower of blocks: "If a tree the size of my thumb fell on the car, would it squish us?"

"No."

"How about a tree this big?"

"Probably not."

"This big?" Arms spread into a huge circle.

"Yes."

"As big as this car? As big as the world?"

Then there were the simple questions that took a textbook to answer: "Where does the wind come from?" Or "How big is the sun?" Or "Why do clothes shrink?"

And other questions *deserved* no answer but still *required* an answer: "Is it bad to lie?"

"Lying is definitely not a good habit."

"Well, what is badder, lying or dying?"

For most questions, I got away with general sorts of answers that neared the truth; however, after a particularly exhausting barrage, I'd fall to "I don't know." Or "Hmmm." Grunt. Or "Why don't you save the next sixty-six questions for your father?"

But some questions were real stumpers. For example: "Are there more trees in Europe than in the city?" Which city? In all of Europe? In a European city compared to a Canadian city?

So to that one I answered, "No."

Or "What do you think they're doing in Ontario right now?"

They? Hockey players? Twelve-and-a-half-year-olds? Plumbers? So because I was hungry, I answered, "Eating lunch."

(Of course, the parenting books recommended that you turn these unanswerable questions around by saying, "What do *you* think?" therefore encouraging the child to tap into her creativity and ultimately do better at university.)

Some questions offered insight into the future. This conversation, for example, suggested then-six-year-old Danica might become a lawyer.

As a simple point of information, I said to her, "When we go camping next week, Nana is taking her van."

She said, "I thought it was Grandpa's van."

"Well, when you're a couple everything sort of belongs to both of you."

"Oh. Does that mean Nana's dresses are Grandpa's, too?"

"Um. Well, yes, I guess so."

"I didn't know Grandpa liked to wear Nana's dresses."

Danica, recognizing her love of The Question, once said she'd like to have a job asking questions. That stumped me for a while—I couldn't think of a job to match the description. Then I became slightly embarrassed.

"Well, I guess that would be a journalist," I said. And silently cursed genetics.

← DAYDREAM →

It was a dark and stormy night. Alone with my young children for the evening, I anticipated the challenge of combining nutrient-rich food from the fridge into something that each child would consume—likely some cheesy noodle mush, although I personally craved a prawn-and-avocado sandwich—followed by the tooth-brushing, face-washing, you-will-go-pee battle, and the rereading of *The Bobbsey Twins* (why did I ever introduce the book series of my childhood?) who, apparently, always ate the broccoli provided by the "slim and pretty" Mrs. Bobbsey.

Ordering in pizza, I decided, would solve the first problem. So there I was, huddled by the wood stove in a baggy, tomato-stained shirt with matching tomato-splattered sweats when the doorbell sounded. I opened the door and took a deep breath hoping to smell Completely Cooked Dinner. But the fuzzy-haired, middle-aged woman standing on the doorstep was not holding pizza boxes.

"Pizza?" I started to say before realizing my mistake. Oh no, this wasn't a pizza delivery. This was a spiritual proposition. "I really haven't time for this right now. Let me show you the fastest route to the neighbours—the ones who have loud parties."

"Hush," the woman said, pushing her way into the house. She peered at the dusty shelves and cluttered floors. (Okay,

I'd worked the last couple of days, and the house cleaning had suffered.) She sniffed slightly and then fixed me with a pair of bird-like brown eyes. "I am your fairy godmother. You will go directly to the bathroom, where you will run a hot bubble bath and climb in."

I eyed her suspiciously. "I'm not in the market for a vacuum cleaner."

She ignored me. "I'll be in with candles, incense, a bottle of Prosecco, a large piece of cappuccino cheesecake, and—"

"A prawn-and-avocado sandwich?" I asked. Maybe I *did* need a vacuum cleaner.

"Indeed," she answered.

As I lounged in the tub, sipping Prosecco and nibbling cheesecake, I strained to overhear the kitchen activity. Apparently, the pizza had been cancelled, and my children were happily eating organic brown rice, three different kinds of vegetables, and a tofu casserole. They adamantly refused dessert, choosing instead to help each other clean their rooms while the mystery woman vacuumed, scrubbed, and folded laundry.

I added as much hot water as I could stand and sank into the bubbles. I heard my daughters in their bedroom, gently arguing about story-time books.

"We can read *The Bobbsey Twins* tonight," the younger said generously.

"No, no," said the elder one. "That's okay. We can read *The Cat in the Hat*."

"Lots of time for *The Bobbsey Twins* and *The Cat in the Hat*," the woman said in a jolly voice. "I'd be happy to read the Dr. Seuss book for the 1,431st time."

"Hello, Momma!" sang each of my daughters as they skipped into the bathroom and spent a good five minutes carefully brushing each tooth. They used soap and water to wash their faces, necks, and behind their ears and peed without the tiniest bit of manipulation.

I was about to doze off again when I heard whispering and felt a soft breath caress my cheek. I woke with a start to find myself in front of the wood stove wearing a tomato-stained shirt. My daughters were planting tiny wake-up kisses on my face.

"Pizza's here," said one.

"Look," said another. "We set the table with the fancy napkins and made you a special card." She held up a rainbow drawing.

I uncurled from the chair and felt a stab of joy as I looked deep into their precious, innocent eyes. The thought of pizza was okay. The house cleaning could wait until tomorrow, and I loved reading *The Bobbsey Twins*.

Sometimes moms just need a little escape, even if it's just a fantasy.

← A TALE OF TWO TEETH →

All the tooth trauma of the past came flooding back when a hysterical teenage Danica called, crying, "My tooth's been knocked out!"

Images swirled in my mind: a painful bloody mouth, a hockey player smile, the size of cheque I'd be writing to the dentist (not to mention the number of cheques I'd already given to the orthodontist).

And so I braced myself for the inevitable drama as I arrived to pick her up. She tilted her head toward the light, opened her mouth, and pointed. I squinted. Really? Yes, a tiny piece of her front tooth was certainly missing, but this was not exactly a jack-o'-lantern smile.

I should have guessed it might not be as bad as anticipated since tooth drama had been part of our world for the past decade. When Danica, age six, first announced that her front teeth were wiggly, I assumed all children loved markers of maturity and started singing "All I Want for Christmas is My Two Front Teeth."

But then I realized Danica was not touching the pearly pair . . . was biting off food with her molars . . . was not even brushing them. In fact, she did not want her baby teeth to fall out. Suddenly the phone lines hummed between my house, Gail's, and the two Sandys' residences as we thumbed through book indexes, looking for "teeth: unusual attachment" or "teeth: when children love them too much" and even "teeth: fear of fairy." But there was nothing.

Since none of her schoolmates had yet lost their front teeth, Danica likely feared the unknown; she absolutely refused to wiggle or even touch those teeth. For weeks they hung by strings, getting increasingly yellow, gums bulging above them. Finally, six weeks passed, the teeth remained, and the school Christmas plays approached. Playing one of the three wise men in the nativity, Danica was to sing a solo verse of "We Three Kings of Orient Are." She also had parts singing and dancing in the school production of *The Nutcracker*. We had already solved the Purrla problem—as a full-fledged member of the Grade 1 class, Purrla would play the part of the wise man's cat. Purrla, who had also rehearsed the *Nutcracker* songs and dances, was ready to "break a leg."

Then, disaster struck. Within twenty-four hours of the production, amid much hysteria, Danica's front teeth fell out in quick succession. We braced ourselves for the fallout. What would she do? Refuse to leave the house? Give up her kingly role (which, most tantalizingly, came with a glittering, bejewelled costume)?

But she got up out of bed and dressed for school. She smiled naturally with us, but the minute she stepped from the house, she developed a new closed-mouth smile and started hiding her mouth behind her hand, her long hair, or Purrla. No one knew she had lost her front teeth. Nativity play? Purrla got a starring role as Danica sang (slightly muffled) into her fur. *Nutcracker* choir? She bowed her head until her hair covered her mouth. Christmas dinner with extended family? She used the new smile and covering hand. No one outside our house ever saw her toothless. She finally smiled naturally again weeks later when her new teeth were about halfway in.

Over the years, family tooth drama continued. Sierra (who, for some reason, looked forward to losing her front teeth) had her first tooth pop out with the help of a teeter-totter. It fell into the dirt and gravel where Danica, Sierra, and I spent the next hour desperately and unsuccessfully searching for it. (However, in one of those brilliant mother moments, I managed to console the highly distraught Sierra by miraculously finding one of Danica's teeth for her to "borrow" for the Tooth Fairy.) Her second tooth came out shortly afterward, and—finally—she was able to place her own tooth under her pillow. (Numbers three and four also came out with a little help, this time in the form of a big yellow slide, where once again we and half her swim team fell to our knees to search for missing pearly whites. One we found in her mouth; one she may have swallowed.)

But on that night, as Sierra finally placed her own tooth under her pillow, Danica, in a big-sisterly way, confided that the Tooth Fairy was actually just Momma. I resisted the urge to put Danica's head under the pillow with the tooth and prepared to face the inevitable drama.

But as I tucked Sierra in, she turned to me with wise-looking eyes and whispered, "I don't think you're really the Tooth Fairy. You don't have time to go to all the little girls' and boys' houses every night."

Ahh, for once . . . tooth trauma averted.

← TALKING ABOUT SEX →

When Meg Hickling's book Speaking of Sex *hit the parenting circuit, I read it and realized that it threw a big pile of dirt on my handy garden metaphor. Children, claimed Hickling, should know reproductive details by the time they attend school. Because I believed almost every parenting book I read, this statement hammered me with horror. Five-year-old Danica was happily attending kindergarten, blissfully believing The Garden Metaphor.*

It wasn't quite how I'd planned it. I intended (having read numerous articles on the subject) to promote early and open sex education for my kids. This meant that when The Great Inquisitor (a.k.a. Danica) began asking reproductive questions at age two, I would calmly outline age-appropriate details.

I would raise sexually healthy children.

Instead, when the question arose, I used The Garden Metaphor: "Oh, the daddy plants a seed in the mommy, and the baby grows in a womb in her tummy."

It worked. It was fine. (Although she gave a rather curious look to the zucchini seeds Derrick brought home from Foxglove Farm and Garden Supply one day.)

After reading Meg Hickling, of course, I understood I had failed. By school age, Danica should have known reproductive details and all the associated scientific names. "Butt," I learned, is not scientific, and I immediately planned to fix the situation.

I read, reread, and memorized Hickling's spiel. I placed Sierra in daycare for an extra hour one Wednesday and picked up Danica from kindergarten. I would take her out for lunch; we would enjoy a leisurely, homey conversation and then, maybe, on the way home, I'd get down to business.

"Danica," I said as the car barely left the school driveway. "Would you like to learn some science?"

I went through the process, using all the correct names, edging through the tougher stuff, and giving the necessary details in as few words as possible. She was quiet for a moment and then asked if that was the only way to make babies.

"Weeell, no," I said, perking up. I then launched into an animated explanation of artificial insemination.

It was over. I had done it. I was a Good Mother.

Then she said, "Momma, can I ask you an important question?"

I gripped the steering wheel as my bravado slid away. *Oh no*, I thought. *Here it comes. It's going to be awful.*

"Why does a car die when the battery dies? Is the battery like a heart?"

I later overheard Danica telling her sister they could stay together all their lives and have babies by going to see a special doctor in Vancouver.

Sierra was four before she popped the question. I was lying in bed beside her and thought she had already dozed off.

"How are babies made?"

Things are much easier the second time around. It was dark and cozy, and I was an old pro at this. I went through the explanation and was feeling pretty good about it. She sighed and rolled over for sleep.

Then came a drowsy little voice: "When will I grow the penis, and when will it fall off again?"

Okay. So practice *doesn't* make perfect.

← FOOD FOR THOUGHT →

A few years ago, as I attempted to send twenty-something Sierra back to her tiny rental suite in Vancouver laden with Thanksgiving leftovers, I realized how the provision of food is such a primal part of parenting.

The offer was gently rebuffed. "I don't have enough arms to carry another bag!" (So I handed it to her friend to carry—ha.) Luckily, I'd dropped off a massive rubber bin full of supplies just a few days earlier, so I wasn't concerned (yet) that she would starve.

But it's primal and it's inherited; I remember leaving my parents' home topped up with leftovers and bits of random groceries. In fact, my mom rarely visits today without bringing a container of home-baked cookies or a bag of coffee that she "just won't use."

Sending my adult kids off with a few groceries is so much easier than all those years of packing school lunches. My lunch-making angst began early, all the way back in the daycare years. For months, I'd gone about the morning routine of packing the diaper bag, a snack, and lunch. I had no inkling I might be causing permanent damage to the psyche of my firstborn until Sue, the daycare operator, finally took me aside.

She explained that all the other children brought their snacks in lunchboxes with little handles, colourful Disney characters, and matching thermoses. Danica's lunch merely arrived in a paper bag, and Sue added she might be feeling a bit left out. I was horrified in the way that only first-time parents can understand. I couldn't bear the suffering my child had silently endured.

Then came the long years of school-lunch packing. Although I worked hard to create lunch-box masterpieces, it was a daily ordeal. The food had to be healthy, it had to be something they would eat, and—the biggie—it had to be available in either the fridge or the cupboards. The more empty the fridge, the more "creative" the lunches and the less likely they'd be consumed.

Some mornings Derrick scoffed at my lunch-box anguish, breezily claiming he could easily throw together a mere lunch or two. I smiled kindly, continued making the meal, and hoped to God that I never died and left him in charge of our children's lunches. In those days, I worked late most Monday nights, leaving him to make dinner. Danica and Sierra did not always appreciate his "gourmet" touch. Once, when he had created some sort of odd raisin, pasta, and pickle juice dish, he set a plate down in front of each child. As she observed her dinner, five-year-old Danica's eyes widened in disbelief.

"This," she said, outraged, "is bullshit!"

It's tough to chide a child for language when you're suppressing laughter. And when I returned home and observed the food, I had to agree with her sentiment.

However, I guess I could have cut him some slack. Just because the provision of food is "primal," doesn't mean it's going to be good.

When Sierra was twenty, she entered a twelve-month fashion design diploma program, which, in retrospect, should have come as no surprise. From the day she set foot in kindergarten, she exhibited signs of fashion "determination."

I've heard some parents select and purchase clothes that their children will actually wear. I used to see these children, splendidly groomed in cute, kid-sized versions of trendy clothes.

It's not that I'm particularly trendy myself, but I always assumed my children would inherit my taste in clothing (i.e., they'd wind up wearing little jeans and denim jackets; maybe a Canucks' jersey once in a while). But Sierra shunned my beloved denim and clung to her own unique sense of style.

The first sign that something was amiss occurred when I took her shopping, and she selected a dress for kindergarten. *A dress?*

"Sweetie, look at these cool jeans."

The dress had a black velour bodice (really, velour?) with little coloured buttons on the front and a multicoloured, mostly pink (pink!) flowery skirt.

She clutched it as we drove home. She found a pair of white tights and a pair of little black (shiny!) shoes and wore the outfit to kindergarten the next day. And the following day. And the day after. And so on. In fact, she would wear nothing else for six months. Same dress. Same tights. Same shoes. I tried luring her with other clothing, buying new dresses, and placing them in visible spots. But the growth of her wardrobe seemed to spur her determination to wear the one dress. Once in a while, I found myself hiding the dress or slipping it into the wash.

"Oh no, I can't find it!" I'd say. "How about wearing one of your other twenty-five dresses?"

Then I discovered *she* was hiding it from me—stuffing it in the bed or slipping it under a carefully placed blanket in her toy box.

Finally, its velvety bodice became threadbare, and she agreed to retire it. I danced a little jig of happiness around the house. A short time later, we attended a niece's birthday party where my mother-in-law excitedly brought out a bag. She explained that the child of a friend saw this dress and wanted Sierra to have it. Coincidence or bad karma? It was an identical dress. Sierra was thrilled; I admitted defeat.

A year later, she attached herself to a single pair of OshKosh overalls; thankfully, I found an identical pair that was one size larger around Christmas time because, by then, she had gone through both knees and was close to bursting through the backside.

Every September, as school rolled around, I thought, *This is it*. This year, she will wear a variety of clothes (specifically, jeans and a denim jacket). But every year she found another attachment.

Shuddering, I sent her off one morning to Grade 3 wearing shorts and tights, big purple rubber boots, and the blue velour shirt she'd been wearing for the past four weeks. But then I stopped short in the schoolyard, stunned, as I looked around and saw the girls in Sierra's class. All of them: shorts, tights, velour shirts, and boots. Sierra's fashion "sense" had apparently caught on.

And perhaps that's not a bad thing to have on your fashion school resume.

As the Christmas season approached one November, preschool-age Danica and I were flipping through an art book, looking at various paintings created through the ages. "Look!" she cried. "There's baby Jesus and the prima donna!"

Obviously, it was a word she knew from having heard it a few times, but Danica wasn't exactly a prima donna. She was more of a drama queen.

When Sierra woke up one morning with chickenpox, Danica—who had a very low pain or itch tolerance—was visibly and loudly horrified. I had to comfort Danica about Sierra's chickenpox more than Sierra.

Spiders were another issue that called for theatrics. Once, we were driving along in the car, and Danica, in the passenger seat, gave a sharp screech.

"Spider!" she gasped.

I glanced over to see the smallest spider in the world dangling from a tiny wisp of a thread on the door beside her.

"It's red," she added, as if that explained her horror.

"It's too small to have a colour," I said.

Meanwhile, in the back seat, Sierra and her friend Kai began cooing. They wanted me to stop the car, so they could collect the itsy-bitsy spider and turn it into a pet.

"Don't touch it," the two younger girls demanded.

"Don't worry," responded Danica, her eyes wide with fear and loathing. "I'm just waiting to take an axe to it."

When we arrived at our destination, Danica swung the door open. "Hurry, run for your lives!" she called. (An axe? Run for your lives? Hold on; stop the show. I'm the funny one around here. Since when did a ten-year-old provide the comedy?)

As it turns out, her dramatic flair has served her well. As parents, we aren't surprised when our children's talents mimic our own. But once in a while, some trick of nature forces us to remember this child is not just a mix of mom-and-pop chromosomes but her own unique being. For example, I'd rather have a root canal than jump up on a stage, but there was Danica, seven years old, acting out the part of the joey kangaroo in the Christmas pageant's presentation of "Six White Boomers."

We watched, stunned, as Danica transformed into the joey. Equally surprised, the choir director lost his place and sent the choir orbiting into the wrong section of the song. From here, Danica went on to play roles like Gretl in *The Sound of Music* and Michael in *Peter Pan*—while I sat in the audience covered in sweat, sick to my stomach with nerves.

Then, of course, there are the occasions when you realize the proverbial child apple hasn't fallen far from the mother tree, and you hear your own words echoing back at you.

This happened the same year that Danica saw baby Jesus and the "prima donna." She was about three, and received a Disney-character doll as a gift. She managed to get out the "thank-you" but then fixed the giver with solemn eyes and said with a dramatic flair, "I'm afraid you have been manipulated by the Disney corporation."

← LIKE MOTHER, LIKE DAUGHTER →

Recently, I read a Scientific American article with an intriguing headline: "Scientists Discover Children's Cells Living in Mother's Brains."

The article discusses microchimerism, where an organism (mom) harbours cells that originated in a genetically different individual (her offspring). The transfer of cells occurs through the placenta during pregnancy and wind up living in the mother's brain. Ultimately, women may have microchimeric cells, both from their mothers as well as their offspring.

This article put me in mind of a camping trip I once embarked upon with my mother and the girls, who were little at the time.

We pitched a big blue tent, and, as nighttime fell, we got the girls off to bed, and then sat up reading under a kerosene lamp before finally crawling into sleeping bags. By this time, a wind had blown up, and we could hear the whip and rustle of leaves above us.

As I lay there, all cozy beneath a pile of blankets, listening to the gentle snoring of my daughters, my mind drifted into the mother zone, where I indulged in a little anxiety. I tried to imagine what would happen if a tree fell on the tent. If it came from one direction, I figured, it would hit the truck—parked beside the tent—first. Would it crush the truck and then land on the tent? Would the truck stop the fall and leave us all unscathed? What if it was just a little tree? Would the tent hold up under it? How about a big branch? And what would I do? How would I rescue my children? Could I drag my mother out from under a tree? And so my thoughts went as I drifted off to sleep.

The next morning, my mom looked a little puffy-eyed, a little drawn, as if she hadn't had a good night.

"Sleep okay?" I asked, wondering if she was too cold or too hot or if the foam mattress wasn't thick enough or something.

"Oh, not bad," she answered. "I had a hard time going to sleep. I kept trying to figure out what would happen if a tree fell on the tent."

Another time, years later, my friend Shari and I took Sierra and Kai on a road trip to Portland. On the way back, we checked into a lovely little cottage right on the ocean on the Olympic Peninsula. As we got ready for bed, I could hear Shari "talking down" her daughter, whose voice sounded pitched with anxiety. Their conversation went on for a while before we fell asleep.

The next morning, Shari, looking exhausted, said she got hardly any sleep. Turns out she spent half the night convincing her daughter there was no threat of a tsunami . . . and the other half, tossing, turning . . . and worrying about the threat of a tsunami.

Even without the intriguing notion of microchimerism, the mother–daughter connection, it seems, is alive and well.

← MOMS ON THE PODIUM →

Amid the two weeks of glued-to-the-TV Olympic sports viewing came a CBC television documentary called *Raising an Olympian*—a look at moms and their roles in nurturing their young sports protegés.

"Schmaltzy," I heard my husband snort at one point, but I was all sniffly-teary so I ignored him. The fact is, any sports mom knows damn well her little Olympian would still be playing in the tot pool without her.

I was a sports mom for years; first swim team, then soccer. This is no small role: it takes fitness (clutch-and-brake ankle muscles); multi-role playing (everything from alarm setter to missing-shin-pad-finder); and creative food packing for all those hours on the road. On the rare occasions when there was no swimming or soccer, I'd stare perplexedly at the stove, trying to remember what I used to cook for dinner.

Swim meets were the ultimate time management nightmares. Beginning at the end of May, we'd load up our bright orange, chlorine-scented VW van and putter to swim meets for the next eight to ten weekends. Each race took a maximum of two minutes. Each child could compete in up to six individual races and two relays—for a maximum total of sixteen minutes in the water. We left midday Friday and returned Sunday night, spending about fifty-five hours away from home for those sixteen minutes. During this time, we found and set up campsites; got to the pool at ungodly morning hours; ensured our young athletes ate the right food at the right times and stayed warm (don't forget the rain) or cool (when the sun blazed); made it to their races; dealt with their losses, wins, or disqualifications; found dry towels; and made sure they got enough sleep.

The summer the girls were seven and eight, we attended a memorable meet in Port Alberni. It started out badly when I forgot a few "essential" items, such as the high-heeled dress-up shoes (apparently so important at a swim meet) and Sierra's special teeth-whitening toothpaste. Danica haughtily explained that the wording on the toothpaste box amounted to pure consumer manipulation, and a loud altercation ensued in the campground bathroom.

Also, Danica's asthmatic cough was threatening to re-emerge, something which could grip her the entire night. She drifted in and out of sleep while she coughed, but the rest of us in the close-quarters of the van needed earplugs, pillows, and thick blankets over our heads to sleep. That night, Danica crawled into the lower bed with me, and Sierra hopped into the top bunk, tossing and turning, jolted awake with each coughing spasm beneath her. Just as things started to settle, Sierra tossed, turned, and fell with an enormous crash, face first, from the top bunk. There was a second of silence—then the wailing began as blood oozed from her nose and mouth.

Danica sat up in bed, wondering groggily, "How can I sleep with all this crying going on?"

I stumbled with Sierra through the dark to the campsite office, where a teenage girl reading a novel stared at us blankly, despite the blood rolling down Sierra's chin. So I hurried her to the bathroom, gently washed away the blood, found her brand new front teeth still intact (phew!), and no broken nose.

The next day she was quite proud of her swollen face and even decided to swim her races. Later that day, Danica fell on the pavement, scraping legs and arms into a bloody-gravel mess. She too swam her races.

And me? After practising sports medicine the night before, I became a sports nutritionist, dishing out timely, healthy food; sports manager, keeping track of towels, swim caps, and race times; sports therapist, counselling my kids through good races and bad; and chauffeur, packing up, hitting the road, and motoring back down Island Highway in time to set the alarm for Monday's 6 AM swim practice.

We all agree: those swim meets were some of the best times ever.

And Olympian moms? You go, girls.

Holiday Havoc

Usually, I liked the fact I couldn't sew.

"Oh, Susan, your daughter has the part of an anteater in an upcoming play. Could you sew her costume?"

"Oh," I would say, sadly, "I'm afraid I can't distinguish the top of a sewing machine from the bottom."

Or—"Momma! My jeans are too long! Can you hem them?"

"Well. I am capable of hemming them. But the stitches would zigzag all over the place; it would take me a year; and, by that time, they'd probably fit."

The simple solution, I would add, is to leave the jeans in the car. Take a day trip to Nana's in Victoria, and "Ohmygosh, will you look at that! We just happen to have a pair of jeans in the car that need hemming, and you, Nana, are the queen of hems!"

Nana would whip out needle and thread and—without any swearing, grimacing, tears, or bloody fingers—hem the jeans in about seven minutes per side. It was an awe-inspiring sight. However, I was not awed enough to learn the trade myself.

This all changed once a year when Halloween rolled around, and mothers everywhere were forced to produce The Remarkable Costume. Sometimes I yearned for the days when my children had less discerning tastes and I could gently manoeuvre them into just about any costume. Snow Queen? Great, we'll buy white and glue on icy-looking glitter. Witch? Easy, buy black and a hat. The Forest Queen? Green and some leaves.

I used to own a string of animal teeth, and, for three years, I suggested at least one child dress as the Tooth Fairy. I even said things like, "A Tooth Fairy. Now that would be a ridiculous costume. I know when I was a kid I'd never have gone as the Tooth Fairy." But because I had a simple costume in mind, even reverse psychology didn't work.

The year Danica was eight, we started musing about costumes way back in September.

"Why don't you be a slug?" I joked and then clapped a hand over my mouth as her eyes lit up and a determined look fell upon her face.

Okay. A slug. Other mothers whip up costumes like this—why can't I? We found a pea-green sheet and bought a metre of Velcro. I draped one of the sheet's fitted corners over Danica's head, took a deep breath, forbade her from breathing, and started cutting.

"Open your eyes while you cut!" she hissed.

"If you're talking, you're breathing," I snapped.

The shape took form. It was time to sew. I sewed and sewed and then wrapped the creation around her body. She looked like a nun in a green habit. So we turned the sheet around, made the front the back, and cut out eyeholes. She looked like a sickly green ghost, and I was getting cranky.

"Why don't you be the Tooth Fairy or something?" I suggested. "We could sew toothbrushes onto a dress and give you dental floss hair." Then I thought about the horror of creating that costume and cursed this problem I have of opening my mouth without thinking.

"I want to be a slug."

So I sewed some more. Halloween is dark, at least. The real problem lay in the school costume parade. Parents (dozens of expert sewers) would be there, and my little slug looked like a child wearing a green sheet.

"You know, I could have chickenpox at Halloween," my daughter reminded me as I sucked the blood from a pinprick on my finger.

"Don't think that hasn't crossed my mind," I said darkly. Her sister had erupted in itchy red spots precisely two weeks before costumed students were scheduled to traipse through school hallways, and Danica was likely next.

However, I'm a Good Mother, so I sewed some more, and when Dad came home, Danica modelled the costume in progress. By this time, I'd added goggles to the eyeholes, cut out armholes (necessary for trick-or-treating), and cut and sewed a Velcro opening on the top for antennae—which had yet to be created.

"Try something around her neck," he suggested. She looked like E.T.

"Let's drape this extra bit of sheet around her shoulders for slime." She looked like a soldier armed against gas warfare in the desert.

That night I lay awake trying to figure out how to make the sheet strong enough to hold toilet-paper-roll antennae. Luckily, the next day I found Martian antennae, which gave the costume a definite alien look. I considered hanging an I AM A SLUG sign on her back.

Two days prior to the costume parade, Danica woke up with chickenpox. Thankfully, she was out of the contagious zone for Halloween night. So after ten hours of costume sewing, there would be at least two hours of costume wearing.

"Maybe next year I'll be the Tooth Fairy," Danica said. "Actually," she added as her face lit up. "I think I'll be a snail!"

MEETING THE COSTUME CHALLENGE:
← ROUND TWO →

The night air hung dark and cold around us, a speck of crescent moon offering little comfort to our frozen hands and shaking kneecaps. The cold did not faze the children, who ran from doorstep to doorstep, their Halloween costumes—the most important items in the world only thirty minutes ago—now pretty much forgotten.

The costume situation this year—twelve months after the slug fiasco—had slid into the comfort zone, despite a last-minute tearing apart of the house for a misplaced mask and the removing of red hairspray from the bathroom walls. But even the Martha Stewarts of costume making had to be impressed with the results of Danica's Halloween wear. I really was clever. While the girls watched a movie featuring Pippi Longstocking, I carefully peeked at the character, noting her distinct hair and outfit. Then I casually mentioned Pippi and Halloween in the same breath. It worked. And when Danica sewed her own patches onto the dress and apron, I felt like praising the heavens. I used a straightened coat hanger to great effect in her hair, braiding her long locks around it, making it stick straight out, and then spray-painting it red.

"So what do you want to be for Halloween?" I asked Sierra, crossing my fingers. "You know, ghosts are really exciting— you get to cut holes in a sheet and wear it over your head!"

"I want to be a bat."

"A bat?" I said carefully, trying to swallow my excitement. "But weren't you a bat last year?"

"Yup."

I held my breath. "We . . . ah . . . might even have last year's costume hanging around somewhere. The one you can even wear with a coat underneath."

"Yup."

"You mean I don't have to sew? I don't have to traipse through drugstores and closets and dress-up boxes? I don't have to cut and paste and plan? Bats are a really, really good thing. Maybe you could be one next year too, huh?"

Suddenly I liked Halloween! We zipped around the trick-or-treating block, the girls picked up several Caramilk bars (Danica doesn't like chocolate, so guess who got her bounty!), and we all did a trip through Salt Spring's yearly Spook House. This was the first year I let the girls do the Halloween horror house, although Sierra, who feared nothing, had been ready for years. She blazed through it, hoping to find something that would scare her, while Danica clung to my arm and squeezed her eyes shut at every corner.

It was a fine evening. And when we got home, I put away the Pippi costume and began working right away on convincing Sierra to wear it next year.

← HOW THE GRINCH STOLE CHRISTMAS →

Way back, when Derrick and I first met in my little office at the *Driftwood*, I should have asked him. Reaching out my hand to shake his, I should have said, "Hello, I'm Susan. Nice to meet you. You're single. I'm single. Things could happen. I need to know. Do you love and honour Christmas?"

As it is, I neglected to pop the question, and the obvious answer didn't emerge for a few years. My children, more genetically wired to me than him during the holiday season, loved Christmas. But we lived with one big, green, hairy, mouth-turned-down Grinch who disliked buying presents, getting presents, Christmas commercialism, and all the season's hype and expectations. Oh, and he hated plastic toys.

Clashes between the Christmas lovers and the Christmas Grinch were inevitable, such as on the Christmas morning when the four of us—Danica, seven, and Sierra, five—had gathered for breakfast. I pulled our traditional cherry streusel steaming from the oven and poured eggnog into fancy wine glasses. Red and green candles glimmered on the table. Looking cheerily at my family, I opened my mouth to speak. Unfortunately, Grinch-Dad also decided to speak and was soon leading a moody discourse on consumerism, depletion of South American rainforests, and the robbing of the earth's natural resources.

Danica, eyes wide, suddenly recalled the worst travesty in her world and, with a few tears coursing down her cheeks, wondered, "Why do hunters go into the forest to kill animals, anyway?"

Glad tidings to all! I hoped the streusel would burn his tongue.

Consumerism sat high on my Grinch husband's list of complaints—hence this conversation one Christmas Eve a few years later as I happily snipped and taped the festive paper wrapping around the bounty of my many shopping trips:

"Next year," he asserted from his observation chair, "we should make all our gifts."

The thought was dizzying as I considered myself making gifts amid driving to soccer practices and going to school meetings and working and house cleaning and attending Christmas plays and doing Christmas baking and Christmas shopping and Christmas planning.

"Time could be a factor there," I said mildly.

"Oh, we can make time. The girls would love new dresses."

"I can't sew, and they don't wear dresses anymore."

"I'm sure they'd wear them if they knew you made them with love."

So I decided to put the question to them the next morning, just before we opened presents.

"Daddy thinks I should make you dresses for Christmas next year. I'd make them with love rather than skill. Would you wear them?"

A battle raged in Danica's eyes. She didn't want to hurt my feelings: "Ah, um . . . I'm not sure."

"Sierra?"

"No way. Can we get on with the presents?"

← CHRISTMAS AND CHAOS →

I began to see Christmas dinner as a microcosm of the entire holiday season.

What took five hours to prepare on Christmas afternoon was eaten in nineteen minutes. What took four weeks of list-making, searching, cringing (as the Mastercard slid out of the wallet again), baking, more shopping, and then stuffing, snipping, wrapping, and Scotch-taping . . . was all over by 9:30 on Christmas morning.

Little pickled extravaganzas that sat mostly untouched on the tablecloth came to represent the entire season's pre-purchase mantra: Christmas only happens once a year. And most significantly . . . my brain started to feel like Christmas dinner's mashed potatoes.

Christmas and chaos were synonymous, and the year Sierra started Grade 1, a subtle, unconscious pining crept over me—something that could only add to the season's confusion. I found myself peeking at the baby sections of different stores before giving my head a good shake and moving on. I was in this tender state of mind when a Salt Spring Island dog breeder brought her latest batch of toddling German shepherd pups into my office.

When a black pup was placed in my arms, just a few weeks before Christmas, I said, "Yes, yes, of course. Absolutely."

And suddenly (after waiting years and years and years to once again sleep eight hours at a time) our nights were broken up by frantic house-training trips outside and little puppy whimpers that said, "Please let me sleep right beside you on your comfy bed, or at least help me crawl up onto the couch."

That year we managed to get through our traditional Christmas Eve with the in-laws, Christmas Day at home on Salt Spring, and finally, Boxing Day at my parents' house in Victoria, a short ferry ride away.

As we bundled into the car to head back home, we breathed a collective, post-festivity sigh of relief. It was over, and things were looking good for a smooth sailing home, despite our car's cramped quarters. Stuffed into the small spaces were several boxes of presents; our aging older dog, Dexter; our small-but-energetic puppy, Magic; two grumpy children; and two Christmas-weary adults.

But things were going well. Still exhausted from waking up at 4:45 AM, Sierra was asleep thirty seconds into the ride home. Even chatty Danica sat silently in the back seat, and both dogs dozed off. We adults anticipated a relaxing ferry ride home, covertly eating chocolates from a freshly opened box, now hiding in the dark between us.

Things took a bit of a dive at the ferry terminal when I grabbed the paper commuter tickets from the glovebox and discovered a mouse had shredded the entire package. However, a little section of the top ticket remained, and the ferry worker seemed to believe that a mouse had consumed the missing portion. (Perhaps this was a common occurrence in the Gulf Islands ferry lineup?)

We boarded the ferry with one child and both dogs sleeping peacefully and the box of chocolates still sitting under the front seat. Then came "the whistle will blow" announcement, followed by a muffled batch of words that ended in "Fulford Harbour."

It turned out that BC Ferries had a special holiday treat for parents with sleeping children and puppies and chocolates. Due to the fog, the whistle would blow every two minutes all the way to Fulford. Sierra and Magic were up by the second blast, the chocolates remained uneaten, and—back to Christmas dinner as a microcosm of the season—chaos ensued in the small car, just like the inside of a dishwasher.

Finally home, we put everyone to bed and fell asleep (until the puppy needed to pee), and I finally rested my mashed-potato brain.

Menagerie

← PETS THAT GO BEEP, BEEP →

These days, you can Google "virtual pets" and find all sorts of information, debates, and warnings, as well as ongoing controversy about them among parents, school administrators, and even animal rights activists.

But back then, it was just a Tamagotchi or, in our case, a beloved GigaPet—and for those of you who have never had the horror of handling one of these beeping, insistent little monsters, you should immediately fall to the ground in humble thanks.

A watch-size computer game offers the handler an irritating little pet, which to grow—even live—must be fed, burped, exercised, and cooed at. Imagine placing a virtual life into the hands of a child who cannot hold onto a pair of socks from one day to the next. But over ten million Tamagotchis have been sold since their debut in 1996.

I confess to purchasing two of the little beasts in one of those air-headed moments. Thankfully, these GigaPets were aimed at young players and had a magical feature: a pause button. Danica and Sierra played frantically with their new toys—*beep, beep, beep*—for about a week until one day (thank God) the batteries died.

But this was not before Sierra, then five, suffered a little virtual trauma with her virtual pet. Both of the girls' pets were based on the story of *The Little Mermaid*. At any given time, the pets were either a fish, a seahorse, a jelly-fish, or a crab. Pets that became too unhappy, hungry, out of shape, sick, or merely petulant disappeared by means of a great hook that dragged them off the screen to Ursula, the wicked sea witch.

Sierra had become particularly attached to her "Crabbie." After all, a pet is a pet. So when the hook dragged off Crabbie, while I was at work, I received a call from a devastated child.

Sob, gasp, sob.

"Sierra, what's the matter?"

"Sob. Ursula g-g-got Crabbie."

"Oh. You sound very sad. Good thing it's just a computer, and Crabbie's not real."

Gasp, sob, weep. "What will Ursula do with Crabbie?"

"Ursula's not really there. It's just pretend."

"D-D-Daddy said Ursula's going to have crab sandwiches for dinner."

"Oh, sweetheart, of course not!" Pause. "Put your father on the phone."

About a year later, good ol' Dad decided to buy new GigaPet batteries. By then only one pet could be found, so after tearing the house apart, I reluctantly purchased another. Of course, the only virtual pet left in the entire universe was much more difficult to look after and, horrifyingly, it had no pause but-ton. Danica took care of it, but unfortunately she had to sleep. Since the pet required twenty-four-hour care, I was enlisted to look after it but could only grasp a basic understanding of how this pet worked.

Hence the scene that drew me back to the first time I let my mother care for baby Danica. I believe the two-page set of instructions included such gems as "If she cries, she might be hungry or need a diaper change."

Danica—patient, but on the edge of hysteria—explained everything I had to do throughout the night to prevent the death of her pet. Sleeping with a twist of anxiety in my stomach, I pulled myself from bed around 2 AM, exercised the miserable thing, and managed to keep it alive until morning. Thankfully, after several more stress-filled days and nights, Danica lost it, and it disappeared forever.

Today, you can find online references to virtual resting places for dead virtual pets and even read about the Tamagotchi cemetery in the UK. You can also check out newer pet versions. They're even more complicated with a face morph component and the opportunity to teach them how to dance and sing together! (Doesn't that sound restful?)

What I haven't found, but which I think is a stellar idea, is an online support group for virtual pet grandparents.

← FASHION: GOING TO THE DOGS →

In the dog days of summer, what better activity than having some fun with the dogs? For example, every once in a while when the girls were little, they'd decide it was doggie dress-up time.

Both of our dogs, Magic and Dexter, proved useful in the dress-up arena. Dexter had already sashayed around the house in various fashions through the years, and once Magic grew, it came time to view the effect of hats and coats and socks on a long-haired dog. So one afternoon, we settled in to relish some doggie fashion with Magic as the star. (Dexter seemed to especially enjoy watching the show.)

First, Magic emerged from the girls' rooms prepared for winter in a hat, scarf, sweater, and socks—tail tucked into one leg of stretchy grey pants. Next, she pranced out ready to exercise at the gym wearing sweatpants, a sweatshirt, and a swimming medal around her neck. My personal favourite was her grandmotherly attire, complete with bathrobe, ribbons, headband, and glasses.

Dexter always had an idea when we put clothes on him that we were joking around. He didn't understand the humour, but he put his ears back in a happy, okay-I-sort-of-get-it look. Magic didn't get it at all, merely looking at us blankly as we giggled away.

When Magic came to us a puppy, it left then twelve-year-old Dexter less enthused than the rest of us. (Although I had endlessly studied the literature on how to prepare our first child for a new baby, the books said nothing about preparing an elder dog for a new puppy.)

Magic pranced around Dexter's feet, slept curled up between his legs, and constantly begged him to play. Eventually, the two worked it out with Dexter proving his superior prowess by flipping Magic onto her back whenever she got too rowdy. Even as Magic grew and surpassed Dexter in height and weight, she continued to consider him too big to take on.

It turned out that German shepherds have the unique characteristic of attaching to their chosen human like a shadow. Magic quickly affixed herself to Derrick, trotting along beside him as he worked in the yard, watching him as he drove away in the jeep, and remaining at the top of the walkway until he returned. When Derrick mowed the lawn, Magic jogged along right behind him—up one side of the lawn, down the other.

Then she discovered the joy of retrieving. Sometimes in those dog days of summer, I'd be sunning on the deck and suddenly feel a presence nearby. A stick would land at my fingertips. Moments later, I'd feel a greater presence and look up to see Magic's black face within inches of mine. Just staring at me, ready, waiting.

But back to dress-up. Dexter so loved the activity, one day he decided to do it all on his own. There we were driving in Victoria, Dexter in his usual spot in the back of the station wagon, lying with some camping equipment we'd just picked up. Suddenly, he sat up with a dish rack firmly attached to the top of his head. We hooted with laughter.

The girls in the back seat tried to pull it off, but it was stuck, and outside the car, fellow drivers and passengers joined in our amusement, laughing just as hard as us.

It was a memorable moment and makes me realize that without children in the house these days, our current dogs have never experienced doggie fashion. Hmm. How would a dachshund look in a bikini?

← A PENCHANT FOR PECULIAR PETS →

For some reason, when the girls were small, "keeping up with the Joneses" meant acquiring pets and, no matter how I spun it, a bowl of shiny, sleek goldfish never sufficed.

Our next-door neighbours on Salt Spring didn't help. They had moved from the city and took rural living seriously, building fences and ramps and little wooden houses, eventually filling them with pygmy goats, guinea pigs, rabbits, cats, a dog, and even a pot-bellied pig called Vicki.

We were more traditional, acquiring dogs, cats, hamsters, and birds . . . although our pets often seemed to have some offbeat quirks.

Danica enjoyed pets well enough but also recognized the extra work they created and could ultimately do without. Soft-hearted Sierra, on the other hand, pestered for pets constantly, and when they didn't arrive, often adopted her own. (At first, the pet hard-boiled egg called Eggy seemed easy enough—no cleaning, no walking—but conflict emerged nightly when I said "no" to Eggy sleeping under her pillow instead of in the fridge.)

Some of her adopted pets caused greater grief. For example, one evening as the three of us girls sat in Sierra's bedroom preparing for sleep, a crane fly floated down from the ceiling and dipped and dived about the room. Falling into their pre-determined roles, Danica screamed in bug-loathing fear and leapt for cover under a pillow, while Sierra cooed, murmured, and immediately adopted it as a pet named Floater.

Derrick, hearing the commotion, sauntered into the room just as Floater buzzed into the open space beside him. Reacting with some primal instinct, Derrick clapped Floater between his hands, causing instant death in the bedroom. Danica's bug-loathing screams stopped abruptly as she realized the horror that was about to be unleashed by her sister. I gasped and drew my hands to my face. Derrick stared in perplexed wonder as Sierra's hysterical screech turned into anguished sobs that lasted forty-five minutes.

Then came the day I caved in to Sierra's pleas at Value Village and agreed to purchase the small blue and white shop vac, which she'd discovered amid the appliances. Her love for it was immediate as she pulled it along by its cord, assuming, somehow, it was a leash. R2D2 became the latest pet, and Sierra and her friend Grace quickly set about washing it ("No, you need to use a hose; R2D2 may not go in the bath with you"), dressing it (how do you dress a shop vac?), and incorporating it into games.

Although it took up a bit of space in the bedroom, I confess I was a bit gleeful about this pet, who did not have to be defleaed or let out at 3 AM. But I should have foreseen the future. Eventually, Sierra became so attached to it, R2D2 needed to go places with us, and of course, I was left to care for it. This resulted in memorable occasions, such as the time I was forced to walk through a park pulling the shop vac by its "leash," or (the very worst) the day R2D2 had to watch Sierra perform in the school play—sitting on the seat next to me.

Eventually, R2D2 went the way of Eggy—slowly moving out of sight and eventually out of mind. And later, of course, the girls became busy with school and sports and started adopting boys instead (which, it turned out, were far more complicated than the good ol' days of feeding, cleaning, and walking pets).

In the meantime, I forged ahead, dodging various stray cats and SPCA dogs, all the while reminding the girls that goldfish are really, really cool.

← **THE MANY LIVES OF PEPPER THE HAMSTER** →

Aside from the fact that many children can't care for a hairbrush let alone a pet, one downfall of giving in to a plea for household creatures is the inevitable trauma of dealing with their deaths. To this day, I recall my childhood friend Sarah and I making the bold decision to skip elementary school as we sat sniffling in her bedroom, awaiting the impending death of her beloved hamster.

Of course, people will insist that pet deaths provide "teachable moments," and there are life lessons to learn, and I would absolutely agree. (In the above scenario, for example, I learned the joy of skipping classes, a lesson that lasted well into high school.)

Getting Sierra a hamster seemed like a good idea until we set it up in the house—which had been quiet at night for the first time in years—and the little monster started scurrying around and spinning its wheel the minute darkness hit. Dexter, a hunting breed, also leapt into nighttime action, pacing outside the girls' bedroom door, hoping to play with the new pet.

Pepper was a furry white dwarf hamster, with beady black eyes and the brainpower of a trout. But luckily, she had several lives. Her first life passed when I rescued her, all stiff and slimy, from Dexter's jaws. I was in the kitchen supervising a houseful of children when some sort of mother-sixth-sense hit me. My brain connected with a soft sound that might have been Dexter in the girls' room.

I dashed in and found our big brown dog with a white fluff ball resting on his tongue. I shrieked—the image of dealing with death and visiting children flashing through my mind—and Dexter dropped the hamster into my hands. Pepper was stiff, almost certainly dead, and I debated my next course of action. Put it back in the cage for discovery later? Deal with the trauma now with all these kids here?

Then I noticed a slight movement. The little puffball was coming back from the dead! Soon Pepper was scampering around my hands. I fixed the cage, which Dexter had knocked over in his effort to play with a fellow pet, and put Pepper back in. One of her lives had passed, and perhaps one of mine, too.

Pepper had more excitement a few months later as I ran the water in the tub, preparing for a bath, and the children decided that since I'd been out of sight for at least five minutes, they should come in and keep me company. Danica grabbed the hamster for additional amusement.

Suddenly, Danica screamed, "She bit me!" and a white ball of fluff went flying through the air toward the tub. As Pepper landed with a splash, I leaped across the room and plucked her from the water. Completely soaked, with pink skin showing through her wet fur, the hamster was about the size of a walnut. Dismayed, Danica grabbed a towel and began drying the hamster-walnut. Sierra, speechless, soon found her voice and, while cooing at the hamster, let Danica know her *very strong* feelings.

Pepper lived remarkably long for a hamster and, yes, her death was traumatic. However, I concede, despite the inevitable ordeals, our live pets created many more stories and offered a few more life lessons than Eggy or R2D2 presented.

← PET SANCTUARY: THE COCKATIELS →

Of the menagerie of pets that came and went over the years when the girls were young, none were quite as memorable as the pair of cockatiels that swooped into our lives.

Their appearance was unexpected given the fact that, in a decade of marriage, I had never once heard Derrick utter a word about the concept of "pet birds." But one spring morning, as the girls and their father chatted, I suddenly picked up on their enthusiasm and excitement. I heard small whooping noises. Apparently, Derrick had given in to his "lifelong love" (*really?*) of pet birds and found a pair of cockatiels. Would the girls like new pets? Duh.

So they arrived. Nine weeks old. Cute. Quiet. Beloved by children and man, grudgingly accepted by mom as "whatever." (I had to work a bit with Sierra, however, finally correcting her enough times that she stopped telling people we had new cockroaches.)

Danica immediately sat down and read the thick cockatiel handbook from cover to cover. I skimmed through it, my horror mounting at the apparent immense responsibility of caring for birds.

The first night we carefully covered the cage with a towel and said good night.

"They need a night light," Danica informed me. "They can't see in the dark."

"Bah," I said. "That's stupid. What do they need to see when they're sleeping?"

Danica set her jaw. "It says in the book that they need a night light."

Sure enough, in the middle of the night, I bolted upright in bed, heart hammering at the ruckus occurring in the cage: wings pounding the air, birds squawking hysterically. It appeared one had lost its footing, taken a dive to the bottom of the cage, and, *without a night light*, could not get oriented. So I got the birds a damn light.

Soon after the pair landed in our home, someone asked, "Aren't cockatiels noisy?" and I said, "What, these delicate little feather puffs?"

Then they found their voices. Once in a while, they'd send out pretty little trills. But mostly they screeched *raaack* and *reeeek*.

And then they began to adore me. The moment my foot landed on the floor from the bed in the morning, they screeched with joy. The rumble of my VW van outside provoked an indoor cacophony of gleeful raaacks and reeeeks.

At the sight of humans, they wanted out of their cage. They pitter-patted around the floor, pecked at candlesticks on the windowsill, marched on homework, perched atop my head, preened my eyelashes, and looked inside my ears. They slowly became part of the family, and it wasn't unusual to read a book with a bird perched on a head or to peek out from under the covers to see a little black eyeball peering in.

Then, as we sang "Happy Birthday" to Sierra one June, we were stunned to hear the male (named Crash—but that's another story) whistle back the birthday tune. I eyed him with more interest: this could be amusing.

I became a bird-talk teacher, and soon he could say all the traditional phrases—"hello birdie," "pretty bird," "good morning birdie"—and also whistle a couple of tunes. I was highly amused the day he finally sputtered, "Want some cockatiel stew?"

Being the thoughtful person I am, and because Derrick hated Christmas so much, I taught Crash a new line just in time for the upcoming jolly season. "Merry Christmas, Derrick!" became his favourite phrase—belted out every day, year-round.

And so the girls' childhoods were strewn with pets that came and went—cats, dogs, hamsters, shop vacs—and with them all the emotions of love, attachment, and hysteria at their parting but not, I should add, a corresponding urgency to feed or walk them or to clean their cages.

Life in the Slow Lane

Living in a small town with kids is different than bringing up a family in the city.

Salt Spring is quasi rural, with a mixed landscape of rolling farmland, forested hills, and polka dots of communities and neighbourhoods. It has a central town called Ganges, which has only ever had one fast-food chain (Dairy Queen), which locals ignored until it went away. There are no shopping malls and no traffic lights. Driving skills seem to deteriorate on island roads. Drivers often forget how to use turn signals; they drive fifty kilometres per hour in the eighty-kilometre zone and then hit the gas to fly through Ganges' fifty-kilometre zone. Periodically the police have to deal with B&Es and drunk drivers. More often they are called on to help retrieve escaped goats or turkeys.

Island characters abound. For example, locals hardly blink twice standing in line at Thrifty Foods behind a man with an iguana strapped to his back or meeting Palu Rainbow Song at the ferry parking lot, flaunting his LSD-trip-simulating gizmo.

The average property size is about five acres, and many islanders live in half-finished houses that drive building inspectors crazy. The ten thousand people who live permanently on the island find reasons (like tending to their pot plants) to stay home during the summer when tourists roll off the ferries, the float planes, and the boats in the harbour.

Many people cannot live on the island. They love it, and then they leave it. Every year, dozens of couples pack up their city homes, hop into their shiny SUVs, and follow the moving van to Salt Spring or one of the smaller Gulf Islands, planning to get back to the earth or indulge in a life guided by "island time." (This is a real concept. Island time means a plumber organized for Thursday at 2 PM *might* turn up sometime the following Tuesday. He might call and announce his slip into island time, but most likely he will not. And chances are good he won't show up at all.) These couples get here, and, after about a year, discover they have found independence, usually in the arms of someone else—same sex or not. A common island joke, which most locals don't even bother to laugh at, is: "What's the definition of confusion?" Answer: "Father's Day on Salt Spring."

Islanders wear island garb—casual to the max and not the least bit fashionable—and drive island cars that rattle and shake and blast over great crevices in the roads known as potholes. Most of the long, forested driveways aren't paved so, depending on the time of year, island vehicles are covered with either a fine layer of dust or a thick coating of mud.

When my girls were young, we islanders were particularity noticeable when we travelled off-island en masse to a soccer tournament, for example. We'd arrive at the park in an army of battered cars and look blankly at the crush of vehicles squeezed neatly into parallel parking spots. We had our own method of parking and it wasn't parallel. We'd nose vehicles into bushy bits on the side of the road or angle them into areas facing the opposite direction. Although these days most of us lock up our cars, it used to be flustering at off-island events when we were faced with the foreign process of removing keys from our ignitions and locking the doors.

Travelling to the city was always an adventure for my country-bumpkin offspring, and it took a long time for them to stop referring to elevators and escalators as "rides," but that's what happens when Salt Spring meets the city.

← TWO MEN, ONE NAME →

It began with a phone message: "Hello. My name is Derek Lundy, and I hear yours is too." Torontonian Derek Lundy, author of the bestselling *Godforsaken Sea*, was on the west coast promoting his book when he decided to dig up a little family history and check out his ancestor Benjamin Lundy's homestead on Salt Spring (ironically, at the time, the home of Frances, the girls' beloved kindergarten teacher).

When he announced his name at the Seabreeze Inne, he received the first of many quizzical, startled, or downright disbelieving looks. He was informed of Salt Spring's Derrick Lundy and called our home.

A lunch date was arranged—I had the privilege of sipping beer at Moby's Pub with two Derrick/Derek Lundys—and the two men determined that although they are not all part of one big, happy Lundy family, they did have things in common, including seven-year-old daughters.

Derek, his wife Christine, and daughter Sarah were looking for a place to retreat for ten months (although, as often happens on this island, they are still here more than twenty-one years later). The new Lundys set about finding a rental home and registered their daughter at a local school, where the two Derrick/Derek Lundy girls—Danica and Sarah—landed in the same class and became close friends.

At the time, Derrick and I were somewhat high profile on the island, since both of us worked at the newspaper. And as the newspaper's photographer, Derrick was everywhere, from house fires to the Legion meat draw. People even dressed up as him at Halloween, donning his trademark black clothing, hat, and braided ponytail.

So when the visiting Lundy family arrived for a dinner reservation at a Salt Spring restaurant, the host stared at them in disbelief, confessing that she'd wondered why the "Derrick Lundy" reservation was for three Lundys rather than four.

But the fun really started when the Lundys moved in. The courier was the first close call. Derek caught him backing out of the driveway, material undelivered. The courier knew darn well that Derrick Lundy didn't live on Morningside Drive, and besides, he couldn't see Derrick's Jeep parked anywhere outside. It took several minutes for Derek to convince the courier to leave him the package.

When Derek gave his name at an island bank, the teller gave him a dark look that said, "What the heck is going on here!" (If you're going to try to con the bank, at least pick a name that no one knows.) Normally, Derek answered business phone calls with, "Hello, Derek Lundy." He quickly reverted to just "Hello."

Once, the two Derrick/Dereks were standing together at the fall fair when Derek Lundy was paged. The two men looked at each other, shrugged, and tramped into the building together, announcing, "Here we are."

The situation became more complex another year in the dying hours of the fair when someone approached and informed me the happy news: after spending a large fortune on fall fair raffle tickets over the years, Derrick had finally won a prize—a spectacular quilt from the 4-H Club! I happily danced over to the 4-H booth, where I learned that the quilt had already been dropped off for Derrick at the newspaper office. I took the quilt home where we all gaped at it for a few hours. Then a misgiving began to creep in—had the other Derek actually won it? Derrick summed up his opinion by saying, "It's the luck of the Lundys. He's lucky if he won it, but I'm more lucky because I have it."

So I called the 4-H Club and explained the Derek/Derrick thing. "Well, it was a 653 phone number on the ticket . . . Cusheon Lake Road is 653, isn't it?" No, no, no! Sigh. So we handed over the damn quilt.

Over the years, Derek has written more bestselling books, and Derrick has taken a gazillion more photographs, and, while cases of mistaken identity continue, the island has accepted that there are now two of them . . . especially since a few years later another fellow moved to the island causing further confusion. His name was Robin Williams.

← WHEN COUNTRY MEETS CITY →

Today, both my daughters live in urban centres—Sierra is in Victoria and Danica in New York City. They've each travelled widely—Sierra has backpacked through Southeast Asia, Danica has traipsed around Nicaragua, and both have travelled throughout Europe. They understand buses, subways, and airports. They're city savvy.

They've come a long way from their childhood.

Growing up on rural Salt Spring, the girls were city innocents. For example, once when they were very young, we went with a group to see a musical in Vancouver. Arriving early, a few of us grabbed food in a restaurant and then strolled back along the sidewalk to the theatre. We came to an intersection, and as four solid lanes of cars zoomed past, little Danica looked up with a worried frown.

"I hope," she whispered above the roar of engines, "someone will stop for us."

Since there were no traffic lights on Salt Spring, she had no idea that the stoplight would change, a walk signal would emerge, and we'd simply walk across the crosswalk.

On a trip to Disneyland a few years later, my girls became so enthralled with "rides" on the Canadian side of the trip—a ferry with a play area! A bus! Escalators! A moving sidewalk!— they didn't really need to go to California.

But the girls' first city bus ride was the most memorable example of rural meeting urban. This occurred when, with great anticipatory enthusiasm, we decided to leave the car at home and take the bus to Saanich Commonwealth Pool in Victoria for swimming with Nana.

We raced off the ferry, over stairs, through passageways, up elevators, and into the sunny outdoors to be first in line for the double-decker bus that would take us into town. Everything was in order. We were the first to climb aboard, and therefore got our choice of seats. Eagerly, the girls selected three spots on the upper level of the bus, right at the front, near a big window. The bus engines revved, the girls looked around excitedly—as if it were the launch of log boats at Disneyland's Splash Mountain—and off we went.

The bus motored onto the familiar highway, and within a few minutes, the girls settled into the routine, the excitement of a new experience slowly subsiding. Then the bus turned off the highway into Sidney. And stopped to pick up passengers. And started. And stopped. Danica and Sierra's heads whipped around at me.

"What's going on?" they demanded.

"We're stopping to pick up other people, who also want to ride this very exciting bus."

"But we want to go swimming."

"But we are enjoying this new experience! Isn't it fun?"

They frowned and looked out the window. They sighed with relief as the bus stopped at a light, and they could see the highway again. Then the bus crossed the pavement (which they knew led directly to the pool) and started puttering through West Saanich.

"What?" they cried in unison. "We could be at the pool by now."

Their faces took on a grumpy sort of look.

About sixty minutes later (it's a fifteen-minute drive via the highway), we arrived at the pool, met Nana, splashed in the water, jumped off the diving boards.

"Time to catch the bus back to the ferry," I announced brightly.

The girls stared at me, then turned to their grandmother.

"Please, Nana," they begged with a touch of hysteria. "We'll pay you to drive us to the ferry."

So much for citifying country girls.

← HIS-AND-HERS DRIVING SOUVENIRS →

These days, I periodically have the opportunity to sit in the passenger seat of the car while Danica takes the wheel. This can be an adrenaline-pumping roller coaster of a ride, in which I covertly grip the door handle (similar to the way in which my mother held it years ago when I drove her around) and remind myself to breathe.

Danica isn't a bad driver. She's "destination-oriented." And, in fact, now that I think about it, I believe the neighbours in the area where I grew up referred to me as "Little Hell on Wheels." So perhaps she comes by it honestly.

Aggressive driving is certainly not something she inherited from her father. My grandmother drove faster than Derrick. At times, he would drive so slowly, I'd have to reach over with my own foot to press his foot down on the gas pedal. Sierra drives at a similar "leisurely" pace.

Back in the days when people in BC who drove a little over the speed limit often received a souvenir in the mail, I was sent a photo radar ticket, which Derrick gleefully posted on the bulletin board for all to admire. He'd often remind us that he'd never received a speeding ticket in his entire life (I wonder why). So I confess I was quite thrilled the summer day we were driving from Powell River to Lund when a police officer pulled us over.

"Were you speeding?" I asked Derrick innocently.

"Of course not," he said a bit peevishly as we waited for Mr. Policeman to arrive at the car window.

It turns out that Mr. Virgin Speeding Ticket was driving 60 kilometres in a 30-kilometre zone!

While I gleefully pictured a copy of his speeding ticket posted alongside my photo radar ticket, Derrick attempted to sweet-talk his way out of it. This involved hopping out of the van, checking the cop's radar for accuracy, telling the officer he was a "virgin," and chatting with him for about fifteen minutes.

At one point, a car full of youths drove by and someone called out, "Give the cop a donut!"

I eyed the Tim Hortons bag on the dash and quickly stowed it under my seat—nothing would get Derrick out of this one. The girls sat quietly in the back of the van, apparently cowed by Daddy's slip into the underworld of traffic crime.

The mighty finally acknowledged he had fallen, and Derrick hopped back in the driver's seat, continuing on the journey in surly silence. We turned around after a brief stop in Lund and headed back. As we passed the scene of the crime on our return, we couldn't see the 30-kilometre speed sign anywhere on the opposite side of the road. With a righteous whoop from the driver's seat, Derrick swung the van around and retraced his route of woe. There it was . . . the 30-kilometre sign was lying flat on the ground. The newly avenged driver (who is also a photographer) leapt onto the road and immediately took twenty-one photographs entitled Sign Lying On Ground. As he tried the shot from different angles, a BC Highways fellow drove up and began to re-erect the sign. So Derrick photographed him, too.

"The police will probably think you kicked it down," I mumbled as we drove to the RCMP detachment, where Derrick presented his case. A few hours later, an officer attended our campsite and drew the word VOID through the ticket. Once back home, I was forced to view the his-and-hers souvenirs: my photo radar ticket sitting grumpily next to his voided ticket.

To this day, Danica's driving record also remains untarnished . . . but I can't say the same for the adrenal glands of anyone riding with her.

← JINXED BY DAD →

The girls and I spent summers attending swim meets for a full decade, chugging up and down Vancouver Island and the Lower Mainland in our bright orange '78 Volkswagen (in those years called The Pumpkin Loaf—The Pumpkin for short—or The Swim Mobile).

Since Derrick worked most weekends as a photographer for the newspaper, it fell to me to load up the VW and navigate our way pre-GPS through cities and towns, discover shortcuts, find my way out of not-so-short shortcuts, dodge traffic jams, and locate campsites and swimming pools.

I became *capable*.

But it all fell apart the day we left our home on Salt Spring, on behalf of the local newspaper, to cover a protest at the BC legislature in Victoria. Usually our travels included just us females. But this time, Dad joined us, apparently throwing a wrench into my *capability*.

The day started with a lift of his eyebrows as I hopped into the driver's seat. He mumbled something about my driving making him sick, but I waved him off, breezily indicating that, of course, I'd drive. Despite being one of the last cars to disembark from the ferry, things were going well. We were zooming down the highway, the girls and I chattering away, when, to my right, Dad grunted and tried to interrupt.

"Photo radar," he snapped when he could get a word in. Naturally, he assumed I was speeding.

"No problem," I said, shrugging nonchalantly. But I snuck a look at the speedometer and wondered how I could deter him from collecting the mail for the next six weeks.

"Now that is a real car," I announced a few minutes later as we arrived at a red light next to a Porsche. "But," I said, thinking out loud, "I bet I can beat him up the hill."

I balanced my feet on the clutch and gas, looking between the Porsche and the light. Then—blast off! I whizzed through the gear changes as the Porsche meandered behind us, and the girls shouted approval. Then the driver realized what I was doing, gave a little grin, and peeled out, disappearing into the horizon. The backseat cheering stopped.

"Does she do this all the time?" Dad complained.

Our first stop was a mall. (Dad had purchases to make.) As we got out of the car, I reached for my purse . . . which wasn't there. Okay, so I left it on the ferry.

"No problem," I said, countering his eye-rolling with an expression that said: "This sort of thing happens all the time, and I'm perfectly *capable* of handling it."

I picked up his chunky flip phone (the days before we each had a mobile), and, after some difficulty, managed to connect with a person at BC Ferries, discovering, yes, my purse had been found. (I told you so.)

Shopping for him now on hold for lack of a credit card, we loaded back into the car. I threw the cell phone onto the dash, rolled down all the windows, and roared off toward the legislature. Then came a sharp right-hand turn onto Blanshard Street just as the light changed, and a city-block-full of cars came at us. Horrified, I watched the cell phone slide across the dash and fly into the path of oncoming steel and rubber. Dad leapt like Superman from the car and managed to guide traffic around the phone, until the very last truck rolled by and crushed it like a bug into the asphalt.

"It's not Mom's fault!" chimed my cheering section from the back seat.

"It was that damn truck," I agreed meekly.

The rest of the trip occurred without too much incident, although I mistakenly thought I'd locked the keys in the car. (I didn't mention this to anyone; at that point I would have broken a window and feigned a robbery to get at those keys.) And the next weekend, the girls and I were back in the van, puttering off to a swim meet, with—I swear—my capability fully restored.

Transitions

← ON BEING A MOM →

What does it mean to be a mother, I wondered one Mother's Day when the girls were small. What is the essence of motherhood? How does one define the miracles, small and ever expanding?

Orange jujubes, was my first thought. Being a mom has something to do with eating orange jujubes—no one else wants them. They all want the black and red ones.

Motherhood also has something to do with the first piece of pie or lasagna because it's the one that falls apart. And crusts. Pizza crusts, tuna sandwich crusts, peanut butter toast crusts—all pushed into your hand with other bits and pieces as children hand over their banana peels and popsicle wrappers with an absent "Here, Momma."

(Of course, we could insert "father" here too, since dads are also such a big part of their children's lives.)

Being a mother means walking from the schoolyard with lunch boxes attached to each arm; knapsacks, art projects, and books clasped to the chest; and a discarded coat or two balancing on top of the entire pile, while the children run ahead, light and carefree.

During the baby period, mothering means looking for stroller access on the sidewalk; learning the location of every park and every toilet in any given place; reading *Green Eggs and Ham* one thousand times; singing "The Wheels on the Bus" two thousand times; lying awake at night designing flu remedies, earthquake procedures, and fire escape routes.

Baby and toddler moms live in a world of cutting teeth and nursing bras and playgrounds. A world where emotions live on the surface and just about anything beautiful or sentimental can make mom weep. (When reading out loud, I always made one of the girls take over for Charlotte's death in *Charlotte's Web* because I got too teary.)

Mothers of young children assume things will get easier, their lives will return to normal, and, if all else fails, at least they won't be so darn busy once the kids hit school.

Ah. No. This is when the driving begins.

One father I know particularly well woke one Mother's Day and did not say, "Good morning, mother of my children (favourite mother anyway). What glorious things can I do for you today besides pour you a glass of red wine to enjoy in a steaming bath and worship your every move?"

Instead he said, "Good morning. Aren't you glad I made you a mother?"

Yes. I am glad. Because there are miracles here that no one—not anyone else in the world—gets to experience. Like that first flutter in the belly, that definite flicker that could only be one thing—a miraculous new life.

Then there is the sweet, sweet smell of a baby's head, the tiny hand wrapped around your finger, the whisper of a sweet-breathed "I love you, Momma" against your cheek, the heartbeat of a child asleep in your arms, the absolute unconditional nature of mother-child love, the sudden vision of the world through little eyes that catapults you back in time to your own childhood.

Or how about the exuberance, the excitement, the wonder of a child's first-time experiences? The moments when you realize that you, the teacher-mother, are learning from the child. Or the point at which those rare times alone turn from treasured gems into a feeling of emptiness, like something (someone) is missing.

Being a mother immediately opens your eyes to the bottomless depth of a mother's love. I wouldn't trade it for all the black jujubes in the world.

← AS THE YEARS GO BY →

It happened about a decade after the kids were born.

Gail and I sat at our desks at the *Driftwood,* analyzing our daughters' behaviours within the comfort of a familiar conversation that had occurred in the very same room at least once a week for the past ten years. On that day we were comparing Chloe's and Sierra's moves to new schools and Danica's fierce drive to excel at French immersion. Like so many times before, our discussion helped us distinguish our own emotional attachments from our daughters, and we looked at their behaviours as if they were beautiful tapestries to pull apart, study, and then weave back together, or science projects in need of a term paper. In this way, Gail and I walked a winding path through the ups and downs of toddlerhood and childhood, examining our girls' actions and our own reactions. Now we stood on a hilltop, with their puberty only steps away, and the foreign land of adolescence just beneath us.

"You should read one of those books on perfectionism in children," Gail suggested idly. "I think I have one."

"Have you read it?" I asked, wondering why I wasn't leaping at the thought of delving into a new parenting book.

She shook her head, and we were quiet for a moment.

"I haven't read a parenting book in a long time," I said, my mind flipping over the stack of books I'd consumed in the past twelve months.

She shook her head. "Me neither."

Then it struck us. After years of grabbing books off the shelves to flip through chapters and solve the mysteries of our children, we had reverted to our pre-child days and were once again consuming fiction. Our parenting literature was outdated. New books, new ideas, had been flung into the parenting arena, and we had missed the game. And didn't really care.

It was time to analyze this: Did we feel we had reached a place of lofty parenting wisdom? No, but maybe we realized that something inherent existed within us that, if we listened to it, would help guide us through the maze of paths that made up our daughters' lives.

I had come to a place in my life—and, yes, this could change dramatically as we soon stepped into that untrodden territory called teenhood—where I realized that even if I read and understood all the answers in all the parenting books, it didn't mean I wouldn't repeat the same mistakes over and over again. And also, most importantly, I knew that my kids were going to be okay . . . or not.

No matter what I did, my behaviour, my actions could only influence them so much. At the core of their being, they knew they were loved. I had given them reason to trust me; I had raised them on openness and mutual respect. I messed up; they messed up. But life and love continued. Somehow, this realization dawned on me slowly as the girls grew and found their own friends and their own opinions. We were all letting go. And it was okay. I no longer saw myself as the carver and creator of their destinies. They were in charge of their own.

One day in November 2001, I pulled myself from bed at 6 AM, like I had for many days over the previous three years. I turned on my computer, stumbled to the coffee maker, quickly checked my email, and then opened up the final chapter of a book I'd been writing about motherhood—some of the material that forms the basis of this collection. I wrote, as was my habit, for about forty-five minutes. The impetus for the book was to offer the girls and other close family members a narrative recollection of the past ten years: a photo book in words.

As 7 AM approached—time now to start making the girls' lunches—I typed in another sentence and then dotted it with a period.

I lifted my hands from the keyboard and stared at the screen. I had finished the book. It had been three years of forty-five-minute mornings at the computer, with no anticipation that it would actually ever be done.

And so, I realized, it is with each stage of motherhood. Chapters open and then close. Challenges arise and are tackled; moments of pure lucidity break the horizon and everything falls into place. Some chapters "read" better than others; some are worth revisiting, others do not even belong in the book.

As I stood up from my computer that day, I was gripped with a curious mix of elation and sadness. After years of coaxing words and sentences and paragraphs out of all those memories, it was time to close the book on the past and walk into the future.

My relationships with my daughters would evolve as the ties which were holding us together stretched and contracted, and as we all grew and matured and changed.

Someday, I hoped to become like my own mother: a loving and non-judging witness of my daughters' lives—one who offered up bits of age-born wisdom alongside a solid anchor of support. And I hoped I could walk the path with them, if someday they, too, entered the world of motherhood.

← A SECOND BEGINNING . . . →

Derrick and I parted ways amicably in early 2002. It was heartbreaking for all of us, and I can say with authority that no matter how "right" or "amicable" a divorce might be, it is tough.

Derrick found a new partner—a wonderful woman named Sandra—and they moved in together, so the three of us continued living in the home where Danica and Sierra grew up. It became known affectionately among our friends as The Estrogen Pit.

I dedicated the next eight or so years to the girls—mostly driving them places. Soccer moved to off-island practices in Victoria, Nanaimo, and later Vancouver, suddenly requiring hours-long trips involving ferries. Then there were the 2 AM party pickups and the last-minute, missed-the-bus dashes to school.

The Pit filled up with the girls' friends, plus a trail of boyfriends. They were fun years.

The day Sierra graduated high school in 2011, I gave notice at the *Driftwood* newspaper, where, over the previous two-and-a-half decades, I'd filled many roles from junior reporter to managing editor. It was time to move on! A publishing company asked me to write a book about heritage apples. I knew nothing about apples then—but I knew a lot by the end of the project. Eventually, I started working on magazines with Black Press Media, landing my dream job of managing editor at *Boulevard* magazine in 2013.

Back in late 2008, I wrote a series of stories for the *Driftwood* about a popular island woman named Lorna

Cameron, documenting her struggles living with Huntington's disease. Lorna had moved to Salt Spring with my friend Shari, whom I'd met fifteen years earlier in prenatal class, when we were both waddling about, pregnant with Sierra and Kai.

For years, Shari had told me stories about Lorna's brother, Bruce, who was her friend from high school in Toronto, but who now lived in Calgary and visited the island frequently. These stories ranged from mildly interesting to downright riveting, often relayed as Shari processed out loud some of the issues her friend was going through—mostly with wives, ex-wives, and a few less-than-perfect girlfriends. So, although I'd never met the man, I knew a lot about him.

As I started writing the Lorna stories, Shari mentioned that Bruce was visiting and asked if I wanted to interview him. Nah, I waved my hand. I didn't need another interview.

"Well, come and meet him, anyway."

So the three of us went for dinner. I was charmed. Later that night, I sent Shari an email, saying, "Actually, I think I need to interview him after all." Then fifteen minutes later: "So, I've known you for fifteen years, and you never thought to introduce me to this guy before!?"

Shari responded with a three-page email, thoroughly documenting every little wonderful thing about Bruce (including random points like the way his one eyebrow pops up when he smiles).

My "interview" with Bruce took place at Moby's Pub and lasted three hours. A few days later, we picked up coffees, wandered down to the beach, and sat on the sand, talking. Another three hours went by. Then he went back to Calgary, and a texting tsunami ensued. Our first date took place on New Year's Eve, 2008.

And the rest is history.

PART TWO

My Act 2

Growth

There are times I don't want to be the adult. I don't want to be the mother. I don't want to be the one who must deal with the dead rodent in the cupboard, and I don't want to remove the tick from the dog's head.

However, I once faced both these tasks within forty-eight hours. It all started when I went to grab a clean towel from the cupboard, and there was a tail—a rubbery grey bit of horror—draped over the edge of the shelf. I slammed the door shut and used a dirty towel instead. Then I peeked back in. Yup, tail still there, and a mound of grey that I simply did not want to observe.

And that's when I first recognized the rebellion welling inside. Why do I have to be the adult? Why is this my problem? Honestly, removing dead rodents is ... a man's job. There. I said it. So I called up Derrick, now my ex, and said slyly, "May I borrow your lawn mower?"

Little did he know that when he dropped by the house, I would casually mention that a dead rodent among the towels was not good for the well-being of his children—and could he please remove it? However, before this plan even began to unfold, he pointed out that rain was pouring from the sky, and why did I think this was a good day for lawn mowing?

Fine. I would deal with it myself. I grabbed gloves and a garbage bag and devised a strategy to roll up the towel that the rodent was on and throw it all out in one big grim bundle. But, oh my God, as I started to do this, the Thing rolled off and fell into the corner of the cupboard. I spent the next three hours watching hockey and pretending there was no dead rodent in the towel cupboard.

I will state right now that I did eventually harness my fear and remove the Thing. It was horrible. But then, wouldn't you know it, I got up the next morning and noticed something sticking out of the dog's head, right above his eyes.

For twenty years, I've had various dogs, and I've never, ever had to remove a tick. Again, I rebelled against the very unfairness of being the adult. I turned to the Internet, hoping for some soothing advice like: "It's generally noted that a young person's nimble fingers are much better suited than adult's fingers for removing ticks from dogs' foreheads." Instead it said: "Try to get the tweezers between the skin and the tick's jaws. Be gentle, yet firm and patient. You don't want to yank the tick's body from his head and create a bigger problem."

So I just flat out refused to do it. Instead I made a lot of noise to wake up Danica, who appeared alarmed as I dropped to my knees and begged—slightly hysterically—that she remove the tick. She said no. Then I became wily. I realized I was speaking to someone who had just spent a year as a starving university student.

"Twenty bucks," I said, a little thrill running down my spine as I read the conflict in her eyes.

"Fine," she muttered, returning moments later with a hoodie that covered her head, gloves, and a scarf. I helpfully found and sterilized the tweezers and offered to hold the dog's head while Danica applied said tweezers to tick. Sierra also stepped up, offering to photograph the ordeal. Nothing much happened, although we were fully prepared for the tick to burst off in a bloody gush of tick head and tick teeth and little tick legs.

"Pull on it," I hissed.

"It says to be patient!"

Finally, I grabbed the tweezers, encircled the tick, and yanked. We screamed as it came barrelling out. Sure enough, it still had teeth and legs. Probably one of God's most ugly creatures. Out the door it went, straight into the garbage bag with the dead rodent. Then I sighed and picked up the bag. Taking out the garbage is, after all, the adult thing to do.

← THE GRAD DRESSES →

As I watched Danica walk across the stage to collect her MFA degree, I found myself loving her school gown—also called an "academic dress." How blessedly simple: it's black, baggy, universal.

High school grad dress? Another story.

I've embarked on the delightful journey of "finding the perfect grad outfit" twice, and one of those excursions comes with a moral to the story.

The first time around, Danica—whose previous experience with heels amounted to half-inch-tall soccer cleats—decided to totter down the bleacher steps to accept her diploma in five-inch heels, while the entire auditorium held its collective breath. She had donned a dress that happened to be the very first she had tried on . . . but had chosen only after rejecting the one hundred others that followed.

Sierra and her best friend Kai were adamant they couldn't buy anything in nearby Victoria because *obviously* someone else would turn up to grad wearing the same dress. After they undertook fruitless shopping trips to Vancouver and various other places on Vancouver Island, Kai's mom Shari and I decided to take the girls on a dress-shopping road trip to Portland.

Somehow, we thought it would be easier there.

Shari and I knew the chance of our daughters finding dresses early in the day was unlikely, but there they were at our first stop—a vintage clothing store, yet—totally grooving on their finds. Sierra emerged from the dressing room in a hideous orange gown, while Kai appeared in a black-and-blue-sequined monstrosity.

They were so taken with the dresses that Shari and I became terribly conflicted. On the one hand, the dresses were horrible. But on the other hand, it was our role as moms to be supportive of their burgeoning fashion tastes. And . . . could it be they'd found dresses (well below budget) at the very first store? We carried on for the rest of the day, but the girls couldn't find anything they liked as much as those vintage gowns. It was only as we headed back to the store that the girls revealed—ha, ha, ha—they'd given us an Oscar-worthy, day-long performance, and, no, they didn't want those dresses.

We left Portland with a good story but no bags containing grad dresses.

When they grudgingly decided to try Victoria stores, both girls found dresses in boutique shops in less than four hours. And because the dresses were registered to avoid duplication, no one else would turn up to grad in the same outfits. Shoes and jewellery followed.

And then—just when it seemed the impossible had occurred and we were all set for grad—surprise! It turned out they also needed dresses for the after-grad party.

The applause followed Sierra as she and her two bandmates stepped off the stage, the notes of her first public singing performance still hanging in the air. Her face, caught momentarily in the blue and red lights, glowed.

"Maybe the accident was a good thing after all," said a friend, suggesting somehow that Sierra's new path may be even better than her old one had been.

I considered that statement as images flashed through my mind: the sickening moment I first saw Sierra's bleeding, broken body emerge from the ambulance; a few days later, watching her pass out from pain as she tried to roll over in a hospital bed; and then months later, hearing her soul-chilling sobs as we drove home from her first attempt to play soccer again—the day she finally realized how very much she had lost.

No, I was a long way from saying the accident was "a good thing." For Sierra, too much pain, too much grief, too much loss. For me, the anguish of watching my daughter suffer, the inevitable guilt, the weight of trying to bear a burden that wasn't mine. No matter what the outcome of Sierra's new path, I will have a hard time ever saying "it was worth it."

On August 21, 2009, as I drove back to Salt Spring after a trip with Bruce exploring the northwest coast of Vancouver Island, Sierra, then sixteen, was riding her bike down a steep hill into the town of Ganges. Life was good for Sierra. She was heading to her first day of work, at her first job, wearing a shirt hand-painted by a boyfriend she adored, and basking in the accomplishment of playing soccer with the BC team at the national championships in Quebec just a few weeks earlier.

I got the call as we stopped in Ganges for gas. Had we not stopped, we would have driven past the scene—an image

I am grateful I will never have. But nothing prepared me for the sight of my mangled daughter emerging from the ambulance, thickly bandaged, blood-soaked foot first, followed by a braced body, and a bloody face. Her eyes were glazed with shock, and she thought her leg was broken.

In fact, she had six fractures: shoulder, wrist, hip, pelvis, groin, and toe. She had severe lacerations on her forehead and thigh, and the toes on her left foot were almost severed, requiring multiple stitching and thirty staples. She spent the next ten days in hospital.

The physical healing that occurred over the following months was like a mesh of wires all tangled up with the emotional injuries. The community rallied with heart-warming kindness, sending baskets of food, offers of help, and a house full of flowers. Danica was at her side constantly before she left for her first year of university on the other side of the country in New Brunswick. Derrick spent hours and hours with her.

Eventually, though, the two of us were left alone to deal with the fallout. On my part, this meant endless emails, appointment bookings, and driving to and from therapy sessions with up to eight different specialists. I faced resistance from a girl who didn't really understand the extent of her injuries; an athlete who was used to bouncing right back to top form. And I had to watch her endure endless pain that just never seemed to go away, especially as she pushed herself to get back into sports.

And as a mother, I immediately tried to carry the burden of Sierra's emotional pain—attempting to shield her from the agony of all she had lost. I wanted to fix it for her; I wanted her to be the carefree, happy sixteen-year-old she was prior to the accident. At the same time, I buried my own grief, guilt, and loss.

For most of Sierra's life, our time together revolved around sports, mostly soccer—a sport in which she had attained national recognition. Due to the accident, she had to turn down a chance to try out for Canada's U17 team, as well as invitations to attend numerous university scouting camps.

I acutely missed the social aspect of her soccer games, and I grieved the loss for her and myself.

But underneath it all sat the guilt. I grappled with the fact that had I not been "selfish" and left my daughters on their own while I travelled with my newish boyfriend, it may never have happened. The so-very-entrenched trap of mother guilt made me believe "I should have been there to save her."

Sierra's mangled foot and constant pain left full recovery uncertain. Her loss of sports confidence caused her to lose certainty in other areas of her life. She succumbed to depression and lost interest in socializing beyond her very close friends.

I exhausted myself trying to pump her up, pointing out the small steps she was taking toward recovery, forcing her to go to those endless therapy sessions—all the while sinking deeper into my own mess of emotions. Finally, I realized I also needed help and, through two different women, learned two things that helped me through the hardship.

First, I discovered the concept of personal autonomy. A homeopath who also did therapy sessions urged me to find words that would allow me to separate myself enough to give Sierra room to experience her own situation. I came up with "Only you can choose to work through this, I can't control that choice." At the root of personal autonomy, I realized, is letting go of control.

Secondly, I had a flash of understanding during a reiki session that by trying to carry Sierra's burden and fix every-thing, I was, perhaps, denying her the opportunity to learn her own life lesson. With these two moments of insight, I felt the weight of Sierra's accident lift from my body. By recognizing that I can't control Sierra's choices, I gave her the space to discover what she needed to learn. Not only was I freed from my own guilt and the weight of her burden, I felt a spark of something like excitement for her—the doors were open for her to discover a new life direction for herself.

Her new path didn't turn out to be a fight back to elite sports—the path I assumed would make her happiest. Instead, Sierra discovered a passion and talent for music and the performing arts. And so, almost a year after the accident and still bearing its physical and emotional scars, she stepped onto that outdoor stage and gave her first public singing performance.

"The rush," she said later, "was similar to that exhilarating high that I used to get scoring a goal in soccer."

AN EMPTY NEST PERSPECTIVE:
← GOODBYES AND HELLOS →

Whenever my birdies fly the nest (yes, I can assure all you empty nesters, it does happen more than once), I try to impart a bit of wisdom.

"Remember," I told Danica at the airport as she prepared to fly off to a master's program in New York, "we are all Canucks." (What if she slid into the dark side of New York hockey and started cheering for the Rangers or Islanders?)

"Remember," I told Sierra as she headed out on a month-long road trip to California after her high school graduation, "serial killers can drive white VW bugs and appear nice."

The thing is, fall is a time when parents say lots of goodbyes. There are the smaller ones—hugs and kisses before the school bus rolls away—to the more profound ones (zoom in on this mom, red-eyed, and sniffling at YVR), when you finally wonder, *Is this for good?*

Social media commentary in September is awash with teary nesters watching their chicks leave home for the first time, and I have some words of wisdom for them, too.

These weepy people don't understand that "empty nest" is a misnomer because every time the nest gets empty—and you start leaving the bathroom door open when you pee, walking around in your underwear, and getting used to once-a-week grocery shopping—it's Christmas and they're back. There's a joyful reunion, and then your fridge is empty and your liquor is all gone and the chug of the washing machine provides a constant backdrop to seasonal festivities.

Once you've acclimatized again to a full house, it's January, and they head back to school. But then it's mid-April, school's out . . . and guess what! This goes on for four years, and then they graduate . . . and guess what!

I'm not complaining. I love having my chicks around. But all that social media weeping really isn't necessary. In fact, according to a Canadian Index of Wellbeing survey done in Victoria a few years back, one-third of adults had children living at home, and 37.3 percent of those said their at-home "children" were at least thirty years old.

So, my advice is to keep that liquor cabinet stocked, and prepare to be full nesters once again.

Matters of the Heart

It could be a defining point in our relationship, I realized, as we stood amid shelves of dusty Stagg Chili and Prem tins in the only food store for hundreds of kilometres.

Bruce and I had just driven an hour from a wind-swept beach campsite on the uninhabited northwest coast of Vancouver Island, along pot-holed dirt roads, past startled blue jays, and even a lone black bear standing in mid-road. Foremost in our minds, however, was more than a longing to view this picturesque fishing village: we wanted coffee.

"We" were a fairly new long-distance relationship—Bruce, a Calgary "mover and shaker," and me, a small-town west coaster. Our tastes found common ground in good sushi, dry cappuccino . . . and a passion for nature in its most untamed form. As long as "nature" included morning coffee.

On this, our first trip to the northwest coast of Vancouver Island, we came somewhat unprepared, assuming those tiny red-dot "towns" on the map meant "gas station, grocery store, and coffee shop." In retelling the story, Bruce is kind. He doesn't mention that as we turned off Island Highway to start the two-hour trek to the northwest coast, he said, "Should we drive to Port Hardy first and pick up supplies?"

I waved my hand, looking at those red-dot towns, and said, "Nah, there's a place called Holberg on the way."

I could see Holberg in my mind. As the "gateway" to the newly constructed North Coast Trail, it would have a grocery store with hiker-specific, just-add-water type of foods, and maybe even organic produce, appealing to the back-to-the-earth-type clientele that would certainly be travelling through.

Holberg was actually a mostly deserted former Canadian Forces base and logging camp. The packaged food in the single grocery store had ancient labels and a thick layer of dust. There was no produce. We hurried back to the truck, deciding we had enough food for a day or two. We would travel to the other red-dot town, Winter Harbour, for coffee and maybe breakfast the next morning.

As we soon discovered, Winter Harbour (population of twenty) is not a town but an "outpost"—a jumping-off point for commercial and recreational fishing. We hopped out of the truck, walked onto the dock, breathed in the glorious sea air, murmured about the extraordinary beauty . . . and covertly searched for the sign that said COFFEE HERE. We quickly learned this red-dot town was not a breakfast destination: no restaurant, no coffee-to-go. Just a one-room post office and a dusty canned-food store.

So as I sought out my new boyfriend's eyes across the shelves, I realized this could go either way. His eyes could have an accusatory glint—"I did suggest Port Hardy"—or they could say "I like you a lot despite your questionable map-reading skills."

In fact, we simultaneously lifted our shoulders in a shrug and set to work, filling a basket with cans of chili, tuna, and stew (yes, we remembered to buy a can opener), peanut butter, jam, and sliced white bread.

Most importantly, we found a jar of instant coffee and a little kettle that, an hour later (now back near the beach), was quickly plugged into an outlet in Bruce's truck.

The resulting coffees didn't match the dry cappuccinos at city coffee shops. I have to say, they were much, much better.

← WHEN IT'S MEANT TO BE →

Every once in a while, a bit of serendipity or coincidence occurs that makes you wonder about the mysterious ways in which the universe unfolds.

A few years back, Lia, my associate at *Boulevard* and a former model, was styling a photoshoot with a woman named Jennifer for the magazine's Okanagan edition. Things felt familiar. Had they met before? The shoot got underway, and the photographer captured some gorgeous images of Jennifer holding her two dogs, one of which was an aging dachshund. It wasn't until a day or so later that it twigged. Years ago, Jennifer was working in Vancouver with a pet magazine that hired Lia as a model. Jennifer was able to find the very magazine in which Lia had been featured, and in it she's holding that same dachshund as a puppy! What are the chances?

I have a couple of stories, too.

One of my childhood memories features an incident that took place in the early 1970s as I camped with my family at Little Qualicum Falls on Vancouver Island. As we splashed about in one of the river's pools, we suddenly saw an Old English Sheepdog float by, caught in the current, with its owners running along the bank, desperately trying to retrieve it. I vividly recall the incident because my parents expressed some disgust about it: not so much by the situation itself, but because it was the '70s and the main players were much-maligned and dreaded "hippies."

Fast-forward thirteen years or so, as I sat comparing stories with my new boyfriend (eventually my first husband, Derrick). Our timelines were quite dissimilar. The twelve-year age difference between us meant that in the years that I was watching *Sesame Street* in my childhood home, he and his ex were out there living the bohemian lifestyle. As we chatted, he explained that when he and his ex initially came to the coast from Ontario, they set up a teepee and lived for a few months at Little Qualicum Falls. And—you can probably guess where I'm going with this—they had an Old English Sheepdog. Our paths had crossed many years earlier.

Serendipity struck again when, a few summers ago, Bruce's first wife dropped off a batch of photos she'd been meaning to give to him. He eagerly perused the stack of images, most of which featured him and his kids when they all still lived in Calgary. But one image showed Bruce holding his daughter Jade—who was about seven years old at the time—on a dock at Cusheon Lake, just a few blocks from our Salt Spring home.

"Great photo!" I smiled. But as I looked at it and took in the distinct red swimsuits worn by the two little girls in the background, I added, "Looks like a couple of Salt Spring swim teamers in the photo as well." Then—"Wait a minute! Those are definitely swim team girls! Those are my girls!"

Danica and Sierra were in the background of the image, almost certainly proving that Bruce and I had met in passing at least once in the ten years before we actually got together in late 2008.

As Bruce and I got to know each other, we discovered a number of coincidences. And, although he has one extra wedding in there, our lives have followed similar trajectories over the last thirty-five years. He got married in 1987, about the same time Derrick and I met. His and my first children, Danica and Dylan, were born less than a month apart in 1991, and his second child, Jade, was born just two months before Sierra in 1993.

Bruce and I both have brothers named Craig, and his brother Craig's wife, Sandra, and I were born just hours apart in January, 1965. Even our dogs were born on or about the same day in 2002.

Jade is Danica's middle name. Dylan was also the name of Derrick's son, and Bruce's first wife was also a Susan. And how strange is it that Bruce and Derrick both have ex-wives born on the same day in December?

Who can explain the mysteries of the universe other than to say, "It was all meant to be"?

← A NEW WORLD ORDER →

One Monday morning I got up, braced myself, and stepped into a new world where the collective rug had been pulled out from under our feet. It was the day in 2011 when the Minnesota Planetarium Society decided that the zodiac, as we knew it, was all wrong. They claimed the Earth's axis had shifted in the past three thousand years, and a new constellation—Ophiuchus—needed to be added to zodiac signs.

For years to come, we'll remember where we were and what we were doing the moment it all changed. For me, it happened at the Tree House Cafe on Salt Spring Island on January 29, when someone stopped by our table and asked if we'd heard about a whole new world order.

Silly me, I thought we were about to launch into a conversation on the long-term effects of uprisings in Egypt, but—shockingly—it turned out some genius had mucked about with our horoscopes and decided we'd spent our entire lives guided by the wrong stars.

"Glad I didn't get the Pisces tattoo," joked some guy on the *Globe and Mail* website.

Okay, that's funny, but isn't it the least of our worries?

After going home, taking a deep breath, and Googling "I really want to stay an Aquarius," I discovered I'm actually a Capricorn. Suddenly, I was floundering in an abyss. For months my Aquarius horoscope had promised "new territory" filled with "adventure, play, and travel," and said I'd be "inspired to push through and beyond new realities" and "direct a wise course of action."

Now that I was a Capricorn, my future was unknown territory, not to mention my relationships. With this in mind, I was downright scared to call Bruce, my boyfriend of two years, whose star sign had not changed. We got along so well when I was an Aquarius . . . who knew what would happen now?

"Everything is different," I said when we finally spoke. "I don't know who I am. My past is a lie and my future uncertain."

He didn't seem to understand what I was talking about, so I added, "I'm a Capricorn."

"Ah," he said. "Don't worry, Capricorn and Taurus supposedly make great partners."

He went on in his soothing, albeit a little smug, I'm-still-a-Taurus voice, but I was thinking, *How does he know that? How does he know the love status of a Capricorn and a Taurus?*

Suddenly, I gasped. "Your ex-wife! Your ex-wife is a Capricorn, and look how *that* turned out!"

Another light went on, and I realized Derrick's first wife was also a Capricorn. No wonder my marriage failed!

"That's it. We're doomed," I said. "The only thing certain in my future is the singles' bar."

The new reality forced me to question my other relationships as well. For example, eighteen months beforehand, I had set Danica loose to attend university on the other side of the country, comfortable in the fact that she was a well-balanced Libra. Now it turned out she's a Virgo, and I had no idea if she was capable of living on her own. And what do I know about Virgos?!

It gets worse. Way back, when I was pregnant with Sierra, the doctors decided my labour would need to be induced, and they set the date for June 21. I covertly checked the zodiac and gave my blessing, noting my child would fall safely into the sign of Cancer and not be a dreaded Gemini. Why, when you already have a toddler, would you want a baby with two personalities? It would be like having three children.

Well, you can probably guess what happened. I was forced to face the fact my two-sided Gemini daughter would probably need two different grad dresses as she prepared to graduate from high school that June.

But back to that Monday morning. After I stepped into this new groundless world, I took some deep breaths and attempted to balance my chakras (or something like that) and went to my new Capricorn horoscope.

I discovered that although I'm not "entering a new territory," I'm actually "building upon new foundations." I may not be "pushing through and beyond new realities," but I will "feel more assertive than usual," and my "actions are a mix of strategy, passion, and rebellion."

Suddenly, I felt that new assertiveness! I felt passion . . . and rebellion . . . and realized that maybe, just maybe, I'm better equipped to face this new world as a Capricorn than as an Aquarius. I might as well take each day one horoscope at a time—since it's all written in the stars, anyway.

(And, as it turns out, all that angst was unnecessary. A decade later, I'm back to being an Aquarius, the 2011 fiasco apparently forgotten by most.)

← FESTIVALS THAT OOZE WITH BOOZE →

The sun shone. The calendar said Friday. And we like beer. But really, who needs an excuse to take in a beer festival? The year we attended Victoria's Great Canadian Beer Festival, it featured 82 breweries, a record-breaking 253, and about 80,000 thirsty craft beer lovers.

As Bruce stood surrounded by beer-serving tents, sampler glass in hand, he had a look of happy disbelief that said, "If they'd told me heaven was this good, I'd have died years ago."

Later, after drinking several samples, he mused about the Golden Mile concept from the movie *The World's End*, where one must drink oneself through twelve pubs, from the start of a mile to the finish.

"We could do that here!" he enthused.

Having had fewer samples, I pointed out there were fifty-eight stations, and with four ounces of beer in each sampler, that would be 11.6 imperial pints of beer. It could well be the end of the world for some.

My day at the festival began with a broken shoe, which forced me to partake in the media tour barefoot. It felt weird, but I tried to be nostalgic: "How lovely to be running free in the grass again without shoes."

However, once the hordes burst through the gates and starting sampling, dumping and rinsing, barefoot was no longer nostalgic—it was yuck. Sighing, I left the park, resigned to giving up our parking spot in the shade to go buy new shoes. Happily, back at the truck, I discovered a bag of clothes destined for a thrift store, and in it, a pair of shoes. Unhappily, the shoes were purchased for my wedding, and they sparkled and glittered underneath my denim cut-offs.

However, as it turned out, I needn't have worried about my fairy princess shoes. There was a guy dressed in Star Trek command gear; another fellow wearing a Grolsch brewery bottle-cap hat; and two musicians outfitted as a banana and hotdog, playing an unlikely (but ultimately successful) duet with a trombone and alto sax.

Bruce took his role as "designated drinker" seriously. My affinity for beer has been tempered by a gluten-free diet; however, there turned out to be festival options for me as well. But for my designated drinker, the options were dizzying, and he fairly danced between stalls (the "dancing" did deteriorate as the afternoon wore on).

The golden mile, indeed!

← THE PATH OF MOST RESISTANCE →

It's not exactly "terror" I feel when Bruce announces, "I see a path," but it's certainly trepidation—and with good reason. Over the years, his "paths" have sent us crawling through thick salal bushes, scaling steep hillsides, and, on this day, sloshing along a slick, muddy estuary leading off the beach in Parksville.

We'd woken up early during a visit to the seaside town of Parksville on Vancouver Island to take advantage of the low tide, splashing through warm-water pools and sauntering over sandbars and along the rocky edge of the water. But it was time to return, and Bruce's "path" landed us into wet, sloppy sand, followed by slippery mud that sucked the flip-flops off my feet, and led us through a scratchy, crunchy bed of wild sea asparagus.

The "path" ended at a seemingly impassable body of water, which, finally circumnavigated, led to a wire fence. With a help up from Bruce, I was left tottering on the fence top, unable to jump to the other side without the help of some random bystander, who rushed over to give a hand. Not embarrassing at all. (Bruce, *of course*, was saved by another bystander, who happened to have a key to a locked gate in the fence. He merely walked through to the other side.)

Bruce's penchant for "seeing a path" emerged during our trip exploring the wilds of Vancouver Island's northwest coast. Driving in our truck, we followed the signs to the trailhead of Raft Cove Provincial Park along a road that became increasingly narrow until it was about the size of a footpath—before it opened up to an overgrown parking lot.

Improvements were made to the trail a year later, but the route down to the beach was a jungle of knee-deep mud, downed trees, and impenetrable tangles of brush. The trail frequently disappeared, leaving us battling our way through the undergrowth.

It was here I first experienced one of Bruce's paths. I didn't know him that well and so naively followed him, my concern mounting as we fought our way over and under logs, stumbled over loose rocks, and crawled through the salal. Bruce didn't say a word as we stepped over a plate-sized pile of fresh bear scat, hoping I wouldn't notice. But I did notice, and that had me looking in dismay around us at all the berry-laden bushes, beloved by bears.

Walking a few metres ahead of me on this "path," Bruce suddenly stopped, and his ensuing silence was palpable. I caught up and stood beside him, also silenced as we looked down at the beach. We'd hit a dead end, and separating us from the golden strip of sand in the distance was a sheer, fifty-metre drop.

Some path.

Later on that trip, we got caught by the tide on a different beach, and after climbing a steep, rocky hillside on the "path" Bruce spotted, we ended up back on the sand for four hours, waiting for the tide to recede. Later, on a path *I* discovered on a *map*, we traipsed along a sculpted trail to San Josef Bay—one of the most beautiful beaches in the world—marvelling at the ease of it all. ("We could tow a wagon of beer on this path!" enthused Bruce.)

And so that's why I had to laugh at a photo on my Facebook feed—and not just because my friend Heidi was looking cranky and flipping the bird at her husband, Al, who was taking the photo. In the photo, Heidi is seen edging along the side of a cliff, and Al's caption reads: "It may have been a bit steep." She responded, "It was a hard climb . . . Please excuse the gesture, he got me at a bad moment."

I laughed because I'm pretty sure Bruce has the exact same photo of me, crawling along one of his "paths." And I know that "bad moment," my friend. I know it, indeed.

← HOCKEY: A RELATIONSHIP TESTER →

It's difficult enough being a Vancouver Canucks fan when the Toronto Maple Leafs come to town and their fans take over Rogers Arena with vexing "Go Leafs Go" chants and in-your-face jerseys. But it's ten times worse when your own partner is one of them.

Bruce and I are two hockey-loving peas in a pod most of the season, hunkering down on the couch in our hockey jerseys several times a week to watch our teams play. Twice a year, however, when our teams meet, things get frosty. (One year I hid Bruce's lucky Leafs socks because he claimed the team always wins when he wears them. Sure enough, the Canucks won! Sadly for Bruce, I have yet to recall where, exactly, I hid them.)

But those times when we go to see our teams play live in Vancouver, "frosty" can turn to downright icy, leaving me wondering, *Should we book separate hotel rooms*?

I was horrified at my first Canucks–Leafs home game, especially by my husband's crazed joy, when the Leafs won. But the second time, I was prepared. I would shout "Go Canucks Go!" louder than anyone—namely Bruce—chanting "Go Leafs Go!" I would boo the Leafs player who took out a Canuck in the previous Leafs–Canucks match-up, and I'd pray—palms sweating—for a Canucks win.

And so early one December, we donned our opposing jerseys, avoided hand holding or showing any sort of close affection, took the Salt Spring ferry to Swartz Bay in Sidney, boarded the *Coastal Celebration* ferry to Tsawwassen (grr, Leafs fans everywhere!), and bought tickets for a bus ride into Vancouver. The first highlight of the day occurred upon meeting the bus driver, who jokingly debated whether or not to let a Leafs fan like Bruce onto the bus. (Insert heart emoji.)

Later that afternoon, en route to Rogers Arena, we stopped in at a club that was filled to the brim with hockey fans. Here, we were forced to share a table with two Leafs fans from Kelowna, who turned out to be good people despite their poor taste in hockey teams. Eventually, we all landed at the arena, merging into a swarm of opposing jerseys.

The game had just about everything fans from both sides could want. The Canucks scored first! And second! Then the more-speedy Leafs took over, tying it in the third period to send the game into overtime. In the end, the Canucks slammed home a shootout goal for a home-team win. Although I was a bit happier than Bruce when we left, he was gracious enough to hold my hand.

It's lucky for our relationship that we are both avid hockey fans. And as much as we love the arrival of fall for all its glorious colours and crisp-but-sunny weather, it is the advent of hockey each year that really defines the season for us.

Fall means a stop at the cable office to purchase the NHL package (all games, all the time!). It has me agonizing over my fantasy hockey picks—do I go with my heart (Canucks) or brain (myriad other teams)? We pull out our game-wearing jerseys, T-shirts, hoodies, and our Leafs and Canucks mugs. I Google "Canucks news" three times a day and often know as much or more than the colour commentators. And then the games start, and Bruce rediscovers the high range of his vocal cords and adds some colour to his vocabulary. (It turns out that every single NHL referee is out to "get" the Leafs!)

One year, when both our hockey teams missed the Stanley Cup Playoffs, we said things like "Thank God hockey is over for the season; we'll have more time to plant a garden" and "Life will be so relaxing. We sure won't miss all that unhealthy playoff beer and stress."

We agreed hockey is a silly game, and what's the point of watching the playoffs when there aren't any Canucks or Leafs left? We would experience a hockey-less spring and be much better for it. But then out came a playoff hockey pool, and I covertly selected a team. Then we both placed bets on the east–west final. Bruce pointed out that he really likes Crosby and the Pittsburgh crew, so maybe we should catch a few of those games. I reminded him that back in the early 1930s, the

Victoria hockey team was purchased by the fledgling Detroit Red Wings franchise . . . meaning Detroit is practically our home team. We'd need to watch that series, too. Bruce murmured something about liking the Blackhawks uniform, and I remembered how much I wanted the LA Kings and the Boston Bruins to get hammered, so those games became imperative as well.

Then we went to Toronto for a wedding, and we tried to become baseball fans by going to a Blue Jays game. It was fun! But next thing you know, we'd taken a detour on Yonge Street, and slid into the underworld of the Hockey Hall of Fame. We placed praying hands on the Stanley Cup ("Please come to Vancouver," I implored), and everything went downhill from there. We purchased "merch" at the hockey store and spent the remaining nights at the bar watching the playoffs (except the night of the wedding, when we checked the games via our iPhones instead). Back home, the trend continued; the garden remained unplanted and beer bottles collected in the recycling bin.

So much for a hockey-less spring.

← BABY, IT'S FROSTY OUT THERE →

Having been born and raised on the west coast and spent all my life here, I thought "cold" meant those rainy, mushy-snow sort of dark January mornings when the air punches through your clothes, right to your core, and only a hot bath can warm you up. In my lifetime, I'd seen the thermometer dip to a bone-chilling minus 8 here on the coast, and staying with Bruce in Calgary one winter, I figured I was ready for the "dry cold."

Bruce, who had lived in Calgary for twenty-five years, was amused.

"It's all in the way you dress," I assured him knowingly, as we trotted over to Danier where I purchased a long leather coat that claimed it was "good to minus 40." Thick socks, scarf, hood, west coast hiking boots . . . and I was set. So, thrilled when the mercury finally said minus 44, I begged Bruce to go for a walk with me.

"Well . . ." he said, eyebrows raised slightly, "there's a pub just down the road. It's about a ten-minute walk."

So we bundled up and stepped outside. It was like walking into a wall of ice. Crunch, crunch, down the steps, down the road, around the corner. Dang, it was frosty. I hadn't counted on my eyelashes freezing. Or the air-sucking pain in my lungs.

"Maybe we should go back," I said a little hoarsely. About ten minutes later, I discovered that the best way to enjoy winter in Calgary is curled up on the couch, watching a hockey game, and drinking Scotch.

I changed a bit that winter. Previously rabid about idling cars—how many times did I sigh and switch off the engine rather than sit in an idling vehicle?—I began to see the wisdom in occasionally leaving the car running for a minute or two. Eventually, I even supported Bruce's five-minute car preheat in the mornings before we bundled ourselves in for a ride.

And I actually uttered the words "Oh, it's warmed up!" when the thermometer read 15 below. I walked to the grocery store in minus 22 and learned that, unlike walking in the cold on the West Coast, a vigorous outing in Calgary's cold doesn't warm up the body.

I called for a ride home.

Many people know me as a Salt Springer. I grew up in Victoria, but I've lived on Salt Spring Island for most of my adult life. However, I never realized how "Salt Spring" I was until I went to live in the city.

When Sierra graduated from high school in 2011, Bruce and I spent the next three years living between Calgary and Salt Spring.

Usually we traversed the winding mountain highway between our homes in Bruce's powerful Toyota FJ Cruiser, leaving lesser vehicles behind in the dust (or snow spray) as we zoomed by. But once we decided to take The Pumpkin, my bright orange Volkswagen van.

I vividly recall that drive into Calgary, the battered, road-weary van sputtering along the highway, passed on both sides by rivers of shiny SUVs and burly, powerful pickup trucks. Later I photographed the van parked in an upscale Calgary neighbourhood. (We couldn't get it started that day, ha, ha, but it's not obvious in the photo.) Truth is, the van looked as incongruous in the city as I often felt.

It's hard to put the city back into The Pumpkin—or the bumpkin.

Some differences between living on Salt Spring and in Calgary emerged immediately. For example, walking past people on the island, you get certain whiffs. Could be a "just out of the garden" whiff, "just on my way to buy (natural) deodorant" whiff, or "just smoked my non-medicinal marijuana" whiff. In Calgary, I'd get sweet whiffs of "just stepped out of the shower" or "just spent the morning at the salon." (This did change during Stampede time, however, when I'd get "just stumbled into a table full of beer" whiffs.) And in Calgary, those muffler-booming cars are driven by dudes in shades and the right amount of stubble—not by people who live down pot-holed driveways that eat vehicle-exhaust systems for breakfast.

Driving in Calgary is a terrifying conundrum of mixed messages: there are the speedy lane changes, honking horns, and flipped birds, characteristic of cranky "must-get-to-the-office/meeting/bar" drivers. But, on the other hand, these same drivers stop anywhere, anytime for pedestrians. You need one foot on the gas to maintain the pace and one on the brake for the woman with a stroller who suddenly decides the crosswalk system is too cumbersome to navigate. On Salt Spring, there are campaigns that actually encourage drivers, who are already acceleration-challenged, to slow down. But unless they're at a crosswalk, pedestrians be damned. Islanders stop for deer, not people.

Other differences are more subtle, and related perhaps to the types of events, such as political fundraisers, that I attended with Bruce. Proudly egalitarian on Salt Spring, people don't drop names or flaunt flashy cards; they are slightly embarrassed about personal wealth. Name-dropping was a sport at political and business events in Calgary, and people dropped hints the size of boulders about their wealth.

So after standing mutely at several such gatherings, I became sly. Name-dropping is easy for someone from Salt Spring. "Oh, Valdy's the nicest guy ever." And, "Yup, I've met Randy Bachman." You could tell they were impressed.

Soon, I became even slyer, saying modestly, "Yes, I own a house on Salt Spring." I'd watch their eyes as they envisioned a sprawling, west coast post-and-beam mansion perched on the rocks, overlooking gently swaying sailboats in the harbour. (Missing from their vision, of course, were the ants, the mice, the potholes, and the obvious lack of a house cleaner.) So I got all that figured out.

At first I revelled in the anonymity of the city. For islanders, it's hard to "drop by" anywhere quickly: even grocery shopping becomes a social event. Consider this conversation I had back on Salt Spring one summer:

"Susan," said the woman, pulling me aside at a party. "You may not know me."

Um, yes, that's true. Who are you?

"But I heard that you've met a new man, and you're living part-time in Calgary . . . and I was wondering, how is that all going?"

I found the anonymity in Calgary exhilarating. I could sit for hours in a coffee shop, working away, entirely uninterrupted. I could people watch. I could land at a bar and meet someone who didn't already know my entire life story. (Of course, I hadn't fully considered that for months of the year anonymity in Calgary occurred less because of its population and more due to being unrecognizable under toques, scarves, mitts, coats, and fur-lined boots.)

But eventually, as we returned to the island for Christmases and summers, I found myself basking in the slower pace, the fresh air, the starry skies, and the thick silence of nighttime. And I rediscovered the comfort of community.

There is true solace in being part of a community that understands and accepts you and, that you know for absolute certainty, will support you in a time of need.

Eventually, we realized we needed to pick a home and stay put. By moving between the two places, we never seemed to put down roots. So, in 2013, we packed up the FJ, hitched up an overstuffed U-Haul trailer, and headed west.

There are many things about Calgary that I love and can't wait to visit again: the beautiful and abundant inner-city parks; the riverside trails; the vibrant architecture; the frequent winter sunshine; the endless array of restaurants; the hum of energy and optimism; and of course, my new friends.

But it was good to be back. And The Pumpkin? Right back where it belonged at the end of our potholed driveway.

← FASHION ANGST →

I confess that sometimes fashion confounds me. Take the Calgary Stampede. The first time this west coast baby made plans to join her new boyfriend at a yahoo-tooting, country-and-western Stampede hoedown, several trips to her closet confirmed the obvious: gumboots ain't cowboy boots.

Compounding the issue was the still-newish BF, whose closet contained a stack of cowboy hats (I don't do hats), various pairs of cowboy boots, a collection of big shiny belt buckles, and a row of western shirts. (To be honest, the first time he met me at the airport dressed in Stampede cowboy garb, I covertly checked the departing flights board, wondering how fast I could jet back to the coast.)

My Google search of "What to wear to the Calgary Stampede?" provided little relief, nor did Bruce, who said breezily, "Oh, just bring cowboy boots, turquoise jewellery, and a plaid shirt." (Did I own any of these things?) But I detected in his voice a certain pitch that said: Stampede party wear is Very Important.

Scroll ahead five years, and I was attending my fifth Stampede simply because I now owned a collection of clothes—like my sequin denim jacket and suede dress with tassels—that simply could not be worn anywhere else. I liked my Stampede wardrobe. (But I had yet to don a cowboy hat; there are limits to my time on the bandwagon—or should that be chuckwagon?)

However, the dress code continued to perplex me in Calgary. Anything goes on Salt Spring. Buying groceries? You can pretty much wear anything from sweats to a cocktail dress with gumboots, bells, and feathers . . . and no one will blink an eye. In Calgary, I maintained an outward disdain for the coiffed, Botoxed, Prada purse, and red pumps look. And yet the notion that people might actually be assessing my outfit horrified me. (What if I'd forgotten to remove the Value Village tag?)

And what exactly constitutes "business attire?" I Googled it to discover that business attire means no open-toe shoes and no cleavage. Who knew? I'm pretty sure that on Salt Spring, hiking boots are acceptable business attire.

Ultimately, I never really needed to fret over outfits—people in Calgary turned up in various garb from under-dressed to overdressed (but no bells or feathers), and I usually managed to fall in the middle. But that's not to say I didn't covertly stalk the social pages of the *Calgary Herald*, secretly checking out city women's attire.

Over the years, I like to think my daughters kept me on the edge of trendy. (Stop smirking, girls.) In those days, when I did little else beyond driving them and their friends around, I'd listen carefully to their music and sing out loud little rap phrases to impress their friends in the back seats. (Well, I assumed they were impressed; it's possible I couldn't see them that well in the rearview mirror.)

The most fun I had was picking up choice bits of trendy lingo. Way back, when the phrase was just emerging, I mistakenly kicked a ball onto the field at a soccer game, and as Danica ran by, I said, "My bad." Her face actually blanched;

it was a great moment. Eventually, my daughters prohibited their friends from saying any hip, un-adult phrases in my presence.

But as far as fashion goes, it's lucky the three of us ended up around the same size. Several cool items in my wardrobe consist of hand-me-ups, mostly from them, but sometimes from their friends. (I can't help it if they left their clothes at my house!) I've often found myself assessing the clothes my daughters were about to buy, wondering how they'd fit once they landed in my closet.

But the biggest joy occurs on the very rare occasion when one of my daughters actually wants to wear a piece of *my* clothing. I try not to look too proud, but it's tough.

← TOP DOGS →

In 2013, when Bruce and I merged the part-time house in Calgary into a full-time house on Salt Spring, our two dogs suddenly had full-time siblings.

The dogs, weirdly, shared a birthday, born within a few hours of each other back in 2002. But the similarity ended there. My dog, Austen—a wire-haired pointer/boxer/shepherd-cross, who looked like a wolfhound—had soaring legs that rose to meet a burly-chested, shaggy frame. Smooth-haired, chestnut-coloured Rollie-the-dachshund boasted legs the height of Austen's paws, and his entire body could probably have fit in Austen's stomach. They made an odd-looking couple as they walked or ran side by side.

Austen loved to chase the ball, swim, dig holes the size of small swimming pools, and go on long walks (runs), while Rollie favoured food, sleep, and as little movement as possible. Austen tipped the scales at one hundred pounds; Rollie weighed in at sixteen.

But the moment Rollie took possession of his new west coast home, he ruled the roost. Soon after we arrived, we went on a forest walk with friends and their two German Shepherds. The four dogs bounded happily along the path until another dog approached. It was Rollie—not one of the big dogs—who charged from the pack, snarling and barking and demonstrating a dominance that definitely defied his size.

Austen had a deep, threatening bark, but he was a gentle giant. If we didn't keep an eye out while the boys ate their dinners, Rollie would gobble his up own food and then spring onto Austen's plate. Once in a while, Austen retaliated with a low growl, but mostly he backed off, seemingly saying, "Oh well, I guess the little guy's hungry."

Same with Austen's big sleeping pad. The moment Austen stepped off, Rollie would saunter over, flop onto it, and fall straight to sleep. Austen would walk back into the room, stare at Rollie for a few minutes, hovering above him, and then plunk onto the floor beside the mat. "Oh well, I guess the little guy's sleepy."

Of the two dogs, Austen had the brawn, but there was no doubt Rollie had the brains. Austen had lived in this house since he was a puppy—over a decade before Rollie arrived. But Rollie marched into the house, and within days had discovered he could poke open an exterior wood door by the wood stove. Outside the door, it was too high for Rollie to jump out, but Austen couldn't believe his luck—here was an escape route he never knew existed.

Occasionally something occurred that indicated Rollie was assessing himself next to Austen. He stopped wanting to burrow into our bed at night, choosing instead to sleep on a "big dog" pad. And Rollie, who was in no way selective when it came to food, had always eaten banana. Austen, not so much.

Once when Bruce handed each of them a piece of banana, Austen immediately spat his out. Rollie paused for a minute, eyed Austen, and then spat his piece out as well.

Rollie had always liked to chase and retrieve a ball (usually indoors, in a hallway), but unlike Austen, who had the webbed toes of strong-swimming breeds, he had little time for sticks on a beach. That is, until he met Austen. Still reluctant to actually enter the water, Rollie became a manic beast on the beach, barking incessantly as soon as he put paw to pebble. He never quite "got" the game, though. Austen would retrieve the stick no matter how far we sent it hurtling out over the water. He'd plunge into the frigid ocean or leap off a lakeside dock even before the stick left our fingers. Rollie? He grabbed the stick in his teeth and would not let go.

Rollie was a lapdog. He loved curling up in my lap, and lorded it over Austen, especially when we drove anywhere in the van, relegating Austen to the back seat. But that all changed the day we visited the Comox Air Show and left them in the van for a few hours. We hadn't thought about how the crashing boom of the Snowbirds' jets flying overhead might affect the boys, but we soon found out. As we arrived back at the van and hopped into our seats, Austen bounced from the back with the speed of a bunny and squeezed his one-hundred-pound body onto my lap, while Rollie stood on the floor with eyes that said, "What the heck!"

And as odd a pair as they were, I think they were friends. The day we brought Rollie back, staggering like a drunk on those short little legs after a series of tooth extractions at the vet, Austen hovered around him like a mother hen.

Ultimately, Rollie outlived Austen by just over two years. But looking back, the day we had Austen put down seemed to mark the day that Rollie started his own downward skid.

Rollie was seventeen by the time he joined his big buddy in the doggy afterlife. Hopefully, they've learned to share a pad.

← CELEBRATING MID-LIFE WEDDINGS →

A friend put words to my thoughts as I approached the Shades of White bridal shop in Victoria: "They'll assume you're buying a 'mother of the bride dress,'" she chortled. Fact is, I was forty-nine (and a half) and in a few months would be tying the knot. Again.

There is something slightly embarrassing about second weddings. After all, didn't we both pledge eternal love until "death do us part" once before? And haven't we already walked down the aisle with the loves of our lives?

Wedding plans for Bruce and me took on certain ground rules appropriate to second (*ahem*, third for Bruce) weddings and to two people who spent a few single years between marriages. For example, we decided to limit the number of exes we'd invite to one each. (We both invited the exes who are also the parents of our children.)

We also agreed the event shouldn't replicate features prominent in our past weddings. So, since I was wed on a beach the first time around, there would be no sand in our toes this time. Bruce wore a tux in the past, so he was permitted to wear a kilt this time. And so on.

The wonderful thing about a mid-life wedding is the opportunity to share it with your adult children. My bridesmaids—Danica, Sierra, Kai, and Jade—were all in their early twenties (so no one would actually be looking at the bride; in fact, after the wedding, someone commented on the "super models" we'd hired as bridesmaids). But all four were exuberant about the wedding details and plans.

Hence, during my visit to Shades of White, I used FaceTime to consult with both my girls—Danica was living in California at the time and Sierra was at university in New Brunswick—as "we" tried on dresses.

I had walked into the bridal shop with the intent of looking around and getting a feel for prices and styles, etc. In fact, I said two things to the saleswoman: "I'm not planning to buy anything today" and "the one thing I know for certain is I don't want to go strapless." (Strapless . . . just so stressful!)

I can't manage to buy a set of towels in one outing, but somehow I ended up purchasing a wedding dress that very day—in less than ninety minutes. And it was strapless.

A mid-life wedding also afforded me the opportunity of having my daughters organize my wedding stagette—a concept I found somewhat terrifying. After all, my age-fifty-or-so friends and I had moved well beyond the twenty-somethings' penchant for shooters. We old gals covertly prepared for the event by drinking lots of water, eating full meals beforehand, and even taking a vitamin mixture that promised to reduce hangovers.

And then it began.

"I've got the margarita mix," announced one young woman happily as I wondered if I should add, "And it all went downhill from there."

The scene was a sandy beach near our home. To get to this beach, I'd been blindfolded, dressed in a faux-leopard coat, placed into a car, and then a boat. I had a tiara attached to my head and a bright red extension clipped to my hair. I carried a bell that read Kiss Me. Once in the boat, I'd tentatively tasted my very first Jell-O shooter ("Don't worry, Momma, they're not very strong"), and then, of course, came the margarita mix.

Over the next eight hours, ten women—five young, five "old"—laughed, ate, played games, drank (but not excessively, big thanks there) . . . and ultimately defied any boundaries of age. The absolute best part was the blending of my friends, my daughters, and two other young women into one big night of seamless interaction and fun. We were all just "girls."

But finally, here's what else is cool about mid-life marriages. For the first time at this age, you actually start to view the rest of your life. When you're younger, it's there, but it's more of a concept. As I envisioned the next four decades, I could see Bruce and me—slightly plumper, greyer, with a few more aches and pains—still enjoying travels near and far, drinking Prosecco at the beach, beer in the bar; still shouting at *Hockey Night in Canada* refs; still bantering, laughing, teasing. I could see us dealing as partners with hardships that come and go.

At my second wedding, my best friend would become my companion for the rest of my life.

← MAGICAL MOMENTS: THE HITCHING →

Bruce's and my "hitching" went without a hitch, probably due to my extensive to-do lists. I believe I saw the visual embodiment of the phrase "his eyes glazed over" when I presented Bruce with his colour-coded to-do list a week before the big day.

We were wed on July 26, 2014, in a beautiful ceremony in our yard. Serendipitously, the trailing white flowers on our yucca plants—which hadn't bloomed in three years (and haven't since)—budded and then burst into blossom right beside the ceremony stage just a few days before the wedding.

The sun shimmered, the guests got all teary, and then each of our Craig brothers made everyone laugh.

The bridesmaids all liked their fancily styled hair and looked stunning in their matching pink dresses—no one could guess the torment it took to get four girls in their early twenties to agree on a single dress. Even more remarkably, when the four bridesmaids' bouquets arrived—each looking beautiful but quite dissimilar—each girl, individually, identified a different one as her favourite. Almost implausible!

Although it absolutely turned out for the best to have the ceremony at our house, we resisted this right up until the final month, especially as I envisioned last-minute house cleaning in my wedding dress, should guests decide to traipse inside.

We wanted to hold the ceremony somewhere meaningful to us, but we also wanted to make sure it was different than either of our first weddings (eliminating a church and a beach). Eventually, we decided on a field in beautiful Burgoyne Bay Provincial Park—we even had this venue on the invitations. But after learning the limitations the BC Parks office would impose on us, and then factoring in the task of moving in flowers, decorations, and chairs for ninety people, we gave up on that plan.

In the end, our own five-acre property was perfect. We planted flowers, hung baskets, placed some beautiful rugs on the stage (which was already in place), and restricted access to the house to the bridal party. When we saw the photos, we realized how absolutely stunning the backdrop to the ceremony was; the towering trees provided an almost cathedral-like ambiance.

Bruce and the groomsmen—his son Dylan, his nephew Cameron, and his brothers Craig and Jim—were bagpiped in to "The March of the Cameron Men," and I walked the grassy "aisle" with my daughters to the sound of Elvis singing "Can't Help Falling in Love." Sierra and a close family friend, Carson, sang "our song" (*Snow Patrol's* "Chasing Cars"), both at the wedding and again for the first dance, and Mark, the sound guy, met my wish to blast AC/DC's "Thunderstruck" immediately following the nuptials. The two bands that Bruce performed with—one local, one from Calgary—rocked out as we danced into the night at the local Lions Club Hall, where we held the reception.

The hockey parts were fun, too. We hung our opposing hockey jerseys with their arms around each other above the head table at the reception and included Bruce's hand-painted, table-top player figures with the flowers on each table. In my wedding vows, I promised to still love Bruce "if the Leafs ever beat the Canucks."

We're pretty sure our guests enjoyed the Scotch at the bar because they went through a lot of it, but people really seemed to like the fact we toasted our exes (the parents of our kids) at the reception.

Earlier that day, as I stood with the girls in the quiet house, waiting for our cue (the sound of bagpipes) to walk the aisle, I had this flash where time stopped for a brief second, and I thought, *Holy smokes—all that work, all that organizing—and here we are.*

From that instant, it was like we climbed onto a speeding snowball; there was no stopping the action. I wish I could have slowed down time and savoured each passing moment— but at least I still have the colour-coded to-do lists as happy reminders.

Joys of the Journey

← V-DUBBING CANADA →

"We might as well get this really clean," Bruce said glumly, holding a bottle of Windex to the windshield of my 1978 VW van. "I have a feeling we'll be taking in a lot of scenic routes."

We had just flown from Victoria to Sackville, New Brunswick, to pick up the van—driven east to university the previous year by Danica and her friends—and would be driving it all the way back home to British Columbia.

Our early vision of the cross-country trip changed instantly in the thirty-minute drive from the auto shop—where the van had wintered—to the home of a friend, where we planned to clean it up. It shook and sputtered initially as I stepped on the gas, eventually belching the iconic chugging sound of a VW motor. We lurched forward, merged onto the Trans-Canada Highway, and reached a pedal-to-the-metal speed of about 80 kilometres per hour.

Bruce was what I would describe as a "destination-oriented driver," used to living in Toronto and then Calgary, where he wove in and out of traffic in his powerful Toyota FJ Cruiser, sometimes spewing colourful commentary at "lesser" drivers. On this occasion, he was silenced as the cars whizzed by us on the highway. I could feel his horror.

The van, called The Pumpkin Loaf for its bright orange hue and white high-top roof, had seen better days—especially before it sat for a year in a Sackville snow pile. It had a lining of rust along the bottom, and the 1970s interior was cozy but rustic. We were all surprised it had made it across the country on the east-bound trip, and it seemed audacious to drive it all the way back.

"That's a very 'teenage' thing to do," commented one friend, no doubt eyeing our greying hair and office attire.

But The Pumpkin had character, and, once our cross-country journey started, even Bruce started to feel the vibe. When you get behind the wheel of an old V-Dub, the world changes. You can't go fast, can't think about changing lanes and passing trucks or zooming to your destination. Everything slows down.

The first time we passed another vehicle was on a stretch of PEI highway. Okay, so it was a tractor, but we felt a tingle of excitement. We passed two cyclists and a ride-on lawnmower . . . and then—yes!—we overtook our first car, cheering and high-fiving. Suddenly, we wondered how many vehicles we could pass in the next twenty-one days and set out to count them. We learned to hide our high-fiving cheers because truckers would just smirk, rev up their engines, and re-overtake us. Then we'd have to eliminate them from the count, which ultimately amounted to a grand total of fourteen vehicles passed, all the way from the East Coast to the West Coast.

The slow-moving Pumpkin ultimately caused us to avoid the Trans-Canada Highway wherever possible, bypassing cities in order to take slower, secondary highways. We motored through sprawling farmland and expansive prairies; saw small towns with towering church spirals and drove past rural homes with lines of colourful laundry fluttering in the wind.

Reactions to us varied. Most people our age nodded with a covert roll of their eyes and said something like "Yeah, I used to have a VW van. It caught on fire." Been there; done that. But the kids we met—most of whom were younger than the van itself—treated us as folk heroes. Driving across the country in a VW van? We so rocked, and the van was so cool.

Fellow drivers, however, were not impressed, especially those stuck behind us on narrow roads with minimal passing opportunities. Making it worse, we bought bumper stickers, and, in a moment of misguided giddiness, slapped on a sticker that said I MAY BE SLOW, BUT AT LEAST I'M AHEAD OF YOU. Yes, we managed to embrace our turtle-like progress, but that doesn't mean others did.

Part of feeling the V-Dub vibe was experiencing mechanical ... idiosyncrasies. Immediately upon picking up The Pumpkin, we discovered the signal lights didn't work, unleashing a fun-filled few days of frantic hand-signalling before we could get it fixed. Also, at the time, the van had an archaic point system in the transmission, which many modern-day mechanics (including one in PEI and another in New Brunswick) simply could not figure out. Failing points resulted in a gradual decrease in power, so at times, we'd be crawling up hills at the speed of a jogger. Ultimately, it would just stop, as it did in Terrebonne, near Montreal. (Although Terrebonne translates to "good earth" in English, there was little good about it that day.) As the van shuddered to a halt and died on the side of the highway, we decided to call Stefan, our German mechanic who serviced The Pumpkin back home on Salt Spring. I watched Bruce's eyes widen in horror as he listened to Stefan.

Eventually, he turned to me, and hissed, "He says we need a paper clip! A paper clip!"

In fact, Stefan had correctly diagnosed the problem as the transmission's point system—the paper clip was merely a method of testing it. (Poor Bruce, it did take him a while to love The Pumpkin.)

The van developed another mechanical issue on the trip that was never resolved. The brakes squealed. So anyone who had not actually noticed this bright-orange, slow-moving, rusty VW van on the road did so as soon as we tried to slow down or stop. Hence the scene in Old Quebec City, one urban centre we'd chosen to visit. We arrived on a Friday evening, driving downhill on the narrow main strip, just as trendy patrons sat down on outdoor seats to dine at chic restaurants. Anyone who hadn't seen us approaching immediately heard the high-pitched screech of the brakes. Bruce, who was driving, fought to silence the brakes by pumping them, while I, crimson with embarrassment, leaned out the window and said, "Excusez-moi, pardon, pardon."

A little over two weeks after we set out, we arrived in Calgary, where we were scheduled to attend a wedding. We rumbled into town via a route that Bruce had driven dozens of times. Vehicles hurtled past us, and he gripped the wheel, noting in wonderment, "I don't think I've ever been passed on this highway before." The traffic got thicker and faster. Cars weaved in and out and around us. Finally, Bruce exploded.

"Where are they all going in such a hurry?" he demanded. "It's seven o'clock at night. What could be so important that they have to get there so quickly?"

I lifted my eyebrows but didn't say a word.

A few days later, we were back on the road, taking a less-travelled route through the mountains to BC. Then, amazingly, we were driving off the ferry on Salt Spring Island—full circle from where the girls had left over a year before.

I looked through the windshield, now dusty with the miles and miles behind us, revelling in the memories of the stunning vistas we'd viewed through that slow-moving glass. We had seen Canada as a living, vibrant tapestry, from the rugged, rocky shorelines of PEI and Cape Breton through the quaint villages of Quebec, the luminous lakes of Ontario, the vast and ever-changing skies in the prairies, other-worldly rock formations in the Alberta Badlands, and the thick green forests and towering mountains of BC. Finally—a few days after our return to Salt Spring—we continued our coast-to-coast journey, arriving in Tofino on Vancouver Island's west coast to take in the crashing waves of the Pacific Ocean. We'd discovered small-town and rural Canada—things we would have missed had we sped across the country on the main highway.

Yes. We weren't able to accelerate much over 85 kilometres per hour, but we'd seen a lot of the scenery.

← SAILING DOWN MEMORY CHANNEL →

It's the scents and the sounds that take me back. Recently, Bruce, our friend Julian, and I decided to spend a Sunday afternoon voyaging from Salt Spring to nearby Sidney in Julian's inflatable Zodiac. As we landed at a marina, there it was—the sound of halyards chiming on masts, the creak of the dock underfoot, the slap of water on hulls, the thick scent of the sea.

The ocean is in my blood. I grew up in a waterfront home at Ten Mile Point in Victoria, cushioned by both the gentle and mighty sounds of the wind, the crash and lap of waves on the rocks, and the constant cry of gulls. But it's the memory of the small fleet of sailboats that bobbed in and out of my childhood that is resurrected by the sounds and scents of boatyards and marinas.

Most memorable was our sailboat *Subra* (named by combining my moniker with my mother Barbara's, and causing me no end of grief as a preadolescent girl, suddenly associated with a . . . bra!).

Our decade with *Subra* began on the front lawn, when I was about four. My father—one of those handy guys who could build absolutely anything—purchased the hull of a Gulf 29 sailboat and dropped it into a hand-constructed cradle and scaffolding on our front lawn. (I believe this was a somewhat unpopular choice within our oceanview-neighbourhood.)

He spent the next three years building the interior, from the beds in the bow (my mom sewed covers onto the foam mattresses) to the beautiful little galley, undertaking all the brightwork, and making doors, hatch, tiller, and handrails. The lingering mix of scents included varnish, stain, and fibreglass.

He worked on it during every spare moment—apparently I once asked if he would work right through Christmas Day. Initially, he built a roof on the cradle so he could saw and hammer out there in the rain, but that proved just too much for the neighbours, and an official complaint shut that down.

My mom recalls a time when the two of them were working on the boat, and, with a great creaking noise, *Subra* shifted slightly in the cradle. They both instinctively placed their hands against the hull, as if they could physically stop it from falling, realizing afterward that may not have been the optimal manoeuvre in that moment.

But she didn't fall, and eventually the day arrived when movers lifted her from the front lawn—I remember holding my breath, terrified the entire time—and drove her to Cattle

Point, where she was launched, still mastless, into the sea. We spent many years on *Subra*, visiting Discovery and Chatham islands off Oak Bay, D'Arcy and Sidney islands off the Saanich Peninsula, and sailing to various ports around the Gulf Islands.

At about age ten, I was given my very own rowboat, which I sanded down and painted a thick forest green. I called her *Spunk*. Periodically—in those days before the lure of boys overtook my waking hours—my dad and I would fish off the side of *Spunk* or one of our other boats. He let me "off the hook" when it came to dealing the death blow to fish that I'd caught, but he did make me clean them.

Subra is long since sold and most certainly has a new (less embarrassing) name now. But those days on the water are etched in my memory, destined to whip up like a gentle summer storm whenever I smell the scent of fibreglass or varnished wood or hear the chime of halyards against the masts.

← JOYS OF THE JOURNEY →

One July, we pulled out from the Last Chance Saloon, in the heart of Alberta's Badlands, and turned right toward Calgary, set to traverse a highway that included a *very important* cable ferry across the Bow River.

"It's so cool!" enthused Bruce. "We have to check it out!"

When the gas warning light lit up our truck's dashboard, we didn't think much of it . . . we'd driven seventy-five kilometres once before with the light on . . . and how far could it be to the next gas station? By the time we reached the cable ferry (yes, yes, very cool), we'd driven sixty-five kilometres, and the ferry guy said the nearest gas station was an hour away.

So began an adrenaline-laced journey through the middle of nowhere, as we hopefully identified small towns on the map and then, deflated, passed through mere clusters of farmhouses. (Adding to my personal discomfort was the Last Chance Saloon beer now hitting my bladder . . .)

As we drove, angry black clouds formed in the distance over Calgary. Soon the clouds were overhead, and, in addition to watching the clock, the kilometres, and our frustratingly slow progression along the map, we were suddenly—*kaboom!*—slammed by wind, hail, and torrential rain.

We looked at each other and laughed and laughed.

The truck ran out of fuel four kilometres from a gas station. We called for service, and a tow truck "hero" arrived with five dollars worth of gas and an eighty dollar bill for his four-kilometre drive to bail us out.

This was not the first time we had run out of gas. Twice on our cross-Canada journey in The Pumpkin, we found ourselves running on empty. (Danica was horrified to learn this, noting that she and her friends had *not once* run out of gas on the entire journey eastward across the country. But to be fair to Bruce and myself, the needle on The Pumpkin's gas gauge was constantly in motion, jiggling back and forth around the half-full mark, before suddenly plunging to empty. Danica and her friends had actually *calculated and kept track* of kilometres as they travelled. Good Lord. Where did this child come from?)

Bruce was driving the first time we ran out of gas, and he managed to steer the van off the highway and onto an exit that happened to be at the top of a hill. The van rolled down the hill, we took a sharp left through the intersection without stopping, and slid right into a gas station. It was a thing of beauty.

The second time occurred in a small Nova Scotia town, where we puttered up and down the streets looking for what turned out to be the town's one gas station—and it had closed down. The van died, and we hesitantly went to the nearest house to inquire about a gas can. "Salt of the earth" people lived there! An older gentleman not only gave us some gas he had on hand but took it upon himself to lead us to the nearest (open) gas station.

As we explained that we were driving this battered, speed-challenged van back to BC, he looked at us in slight horror, shaking his head, and saying in a thick Nova Scotian accent, "My son. My son."

The point of all these travel-challenged reminiscences is that none of it mattered. Each time we laughed. We were together; we enjoyed each other's company. All was good.

← INTUITIVE DRIVING →

On the road these days, with our iPhones cheerily crooning out Google Maps directions ("In 200 metres, turn left," says Siri), life is a bowl of cherries.

Not so, years ago, on all those weekends my girls and I packed up the van and headed out on the road, first to swim meets and later to soccer games on the Lower Mainland and beyond.

Often I'd rely on a directional hunch to get us to our campground, employing a sort of intuitive sense of direction. To be honest, this isn't recommended. In fact, the Lower Mainland so completely confounded me that I'd find myself zooming down a highway north when I needed to go south or herded by traffic across a soaring bridge—destination unknown. Once, we set out to a swim meet in Port Coquitlam, and eight-year-old Danica was in the passenger seat, clutching a convoluted list of highway names and numbers and exits and lane changes. The drive involved close to three hours of traffic jams and highway construction and, yes, a few wrong turns.

Asking for directions seemed counter-intuitive to my intuitive sense of direction, but finally, thoroughly lost, I pulled off the highway, and we marched into a convenience store. The woman behind the counter knew exactly where we needed to go and explained everything with a rapid-fire confidence. She was terribly helpful, but as we climbed back into the van, I looked at Danica and asked, "Did you get that?"

She shook her head sadly and said, "Do you think it was Chinese or Japanese?"

But no matter how bad Vancouver might be, I can't stress how confusing the north/south, street/avenue numbered grid system is in Calgary. And just when you think you have it figured out, there you are hurtling down an eight-lane freeway, with traffic merging from both sides, realizing you are driving to Edmonton, when actually you were aiming for downtown Calgary. In the three years I lived there, I discovered the joy of leaving the car behind and walking.

So it was with great trepidation that I watched Sierra and Kai fulfill, at age eighteen, a lifelong (ha!) dream to do a road trip to California after graduation. They planned to go for a month, with no particular destination, living out of the back of Shari's car. Shari and I had *many* objections to this plan, the foremost being our certainty that gun-toting serial killers hung out at most roadside stops in the US (we're big fans of true crime books), and that these two young women (who couldn't hold onto their running shoes without losing them) could meet any number of ill adventures.

"But you'll get lost!" I implored, thinking of all my driving disasters.

"How can we get lost," answered Sierra calmly, "when we don't know where we're going?"

That stumped me a bit. So I bought them a GPS, which they named Floyd, and off they went. Luckily, we didn't hear about most of their adventures until they returned home, but Floyd didn't work very well, and there were familiar-to-me stories of merging the wrong way on a one-way road and arriving at a few unplanned destinations. However, mostly, it seemed they suffered from "intuitive parking" mishaps.

For example, eager to pick up two friends, who were flying into Los Angeles International Airport (one of the busiest airports in the world), they managed to find parking, make their way to international arrivals, and even locate their friends. What they neglected to do was note where they left the car. Faced with seven different multi-levelled parkades—let's just say it took them several hours to find it.

These days, we're all driving with confidence, ready to take on the most complicated directions with Siri's soothing voice. But wait . . . where did I put my iPhone?

Me Time

← THE BIG 5-OH →

Every winter I think, This is the year I'll have a big bash of a party in January.

Then, along rolls my birth month, and all I want to do is cocoon: crawl under the covers with a thick novel; schedule a massage; hunker down on the couch, beer in hand, and cheer for the Canucks. These are my winter comforts.

However, in 2015, it was inevitable. *Party I must*, I thought, because it was a Big One.

A gazillion years ago, when I turned thirty, I wrote a column bemoaning my advancement into a new decade "where I could suddenly see the rest of my life." How ridiculous. As I turned fifty, I really saw the rest of my life—and it was a lot shorter now. No matter which way you view it, fifty seems a decade older than forty-nine.

Things start happening at this age. Weirdly, my husband and I have both noticed that our clothes are shrinking. Shirts, pants, even a favourite belt I've worn for years. All shrinking.

And people don't speak loudly anymore! I've been deaf in one ear for years, so I don't notice it so much.

But recently Bruce said, "The kids seem to be talking quieter these days."

I said, "Do you think it's the kids or all those years you spent drumming in rock bands without earplugs?"

He said, "Pardon?"

Here's another weird thing: often, I've noticed that rooms heat up without explanation. There I am peeling off layers of clothing, and no one else seems to even notice the temperature change.

How about TV commercials? Suddenly, I've realized my demographic is no longer the target market for anything except anti-aging creams and Cialis. Who are all these children driving new cars and trying to get stains out of clothing?

When we lived in Calgary, Bruce hung out on Friday evenings with a group of men—mostly ex-journalists and politicos. They'd chat about sports, politics, and current events. (Never chatted about women, though, nope, and never ogled the young servers either.) One night someone started describing in detail his knee surgery; another moaned about a bad back, and yet another told the story of a friend with a rare disease.

"Enough!" hollered one man. "New rule: just one ailment per meeting."

Despite all this, I figured that by the time my Big One actually happened in January, I'd be ready to embrace it. These are, in fact, pretty good years, and it's more about how the big 5-OH sounds than how it feels. So I'd do it—I'd shed the cocoon long enough to celebrate and turn up the heat on winter.

In fact, I did turn up the heat—I spent my birthday lying on the couch with a flu fever. (Where are the TV ads advertising flu remedies for fifty-year-olds? Even these actors look like children.) So, in the end, my party was pushed to February, and I continued with a clean record of January cocooning.

Apparently, I look a little like the actress Blythe Danner.

I've heard the comparison before and accepted it with amusement—she is after all twenty years my senior—but during a trip to New York City, I had the unexpected experience of walking a few steps in Blythe's heels.

It started at the star-studded Tribeca Ball, a fundraiser for the New York Academy of Art, where Danica attended grad school. It's a big deal, attended by numerous celebrities, and as I reached in for my second glass of champagne, a man in a gleaming suit stopped and studied me.

"You look a lot like Blythe Danner," he said. "And I should know; I've met her six times."

A few minutes later, someone in the stairwell said, "Hi Blythe." And toward the end of the evening, some young man dragged me off to pose in a photo with him.

But things got even stranger as our small group of five shimmied in our sleek outfits over to the nearby Roxy Hotel for a drink and bite to eat. My (fake!) diamond earrings must have glimmered as we sat down in the dimly lit lounge because a hush fell over the staff, and our Prosecco and frites were delivered with surprising deference.

"If there is anything you need . . ." the server said.

To our right sat a drunken couple from Belarus. Suddenly, the woman launched herself toward us, clutching me in a hug, and saying in a thick Belarusian accent, "My husband told me not to bother the celebrity, but I had to come and meet you."

She continued to chat with everyone at our table, periodically stopping mid-sentence to plant a kiss on my cheek. Her husband ordered a round of vodka and began dropping loud hints about the Tribeca Ball's after-party. Perhaps we could get them into it?

The Belarusian woman's accosting of me alarmed the staff, and quite a ruckus ensued. Eventually, I excused myself and escaped downstairs to the bathroom. Later, as I stood in the hallway, heart beating, not wanting to go back into the lounge, I realized I was unwittingly experiencing the life of a celebrity. I didn't like it!

This celebrity-worshipping seemed out of place in a city that epitomizes defiant individualism. But this was actually our second brush of the day with it—and the first was also highly amusing.

As we explored the spectacular interior of St. Patrick's Cathedral, I pointed at a photo of Pope Francis on the wall. It's a bit of a family joke that Bruce has similar expressions and facial structure to the Pope, and we often amuse ourselves by Googling images of Pope Francis and comparing them to Bruce. So I directed him to stand under the photo while I pulled out my camera to snap a picture.

Suddenly a crowd of Italians appeared. They all wanted photos of Bruce and the Pope! The rest of us burst from the church laughing as Bruce posed for photos.

Later on the same trip, Danica and I landed at a heavily crowded bar in trendy Williamsburg, where we were guided to seats squeezed into the back of a secondary room. Here we each ordered a glass of Cava.

As we tucked into conversation, I peripherally noticed some sort of mild commotion happening among the staff but didn't pay much attention. The next thing you know, the owner of the place had sidled up to the table, introduced himself, and offered us seating at the front of the bar—the window seat, in fact! I waved my hand and said, "Thanks, but we're perfectly comfortable." Moments later the server appeared, but instead of delivering us the typical two glasses of bubbly, he had a brand new bottle in hand. He opened it with a flourish before grandly pouring it out for us. I felt so bad for them when I brought out my "Susan Lundy" credit card to pay for it all.

I've been asked so many times if I'm Blythe that I've started to wonder what her response is to the question. Does she fess up? Or does she say, "Blythe who?" At any rate, I'm happy to walk in my own shoes. The heels of a celebrity feel a little uncomfortable.

← BEATING THE WINTER BLUES →

I'm not sure how to define the winter blues, but I'm certain they occur in February when everyone you know is in the Caribbean or Hawai'i, and you're staring out the window (which needs washing) at a wet, muddy backyard that you can hardly see because of the steady stream of rain and gloom.

Recently I tried to book myself a February flight to Calgary for some work but ended up searching WestJet vacations instead. Also, I found myself procrastinating more than usual on tasks that put me outdoors—dashing from store to car—or activities that required heels instead of gumboots. These are the winter blues.

One February, we did escape. A "go at the last minute" deal landed in my inbox touting a Huatulco vacation on the exact (and only) days I could squeeze out some holiday time. Before I knew it, I'd clicked all the boxes, pulled out the credit card, and . . . we were going to Mexico! I sat back and looked at the screen, stunned and yet thrilled by my uncharacteristic lack of planning and prudence.

It was our first all-inclusive holiday, and while it's not typically the way we like to travel, let me say that taking six days out of an exhausting work schedule in February to lie on the sand, bounce around in warm waves, drink piña coladas at 11 AM, and read copious amounts of fiction is the absolute antidote to the winter blues.

Closer to home, we've beat seasonal doldrums by embracing short excursions to Sooke or Tofino. This means switching off the iPhones (most difficult), dressing in rain gear for wet walks on the beach, and cozying up by the fireplace, amid sips of Prosecco and trips to the outdoor hot tub.

I have another less traditional winter ritual. I like to purge the house. For years, every January, I eliminated one hundred items. My daughters picked up on it, and it became three hundred items. Joy!

Once in my enthusiasm, however, I purged some of my then-husband Derrick's clothes. To my credit, I showed him the bundle that was heading out the door . . . but perhaps he didn't look that closely. A few months later, he came home after perusing a nearby thrift shop, excited about this beautiful white shirt he'd found. He put it on to show me and discovered a cancelled cheque in the pocket. His cheque. His former shirt. (It's no wonder, really, that I became his ex.)

For many years—when I had nary a husband in sight—my shelves gleamed with the absence of "things." But then Bruce and I combined two homes into one, and I suddenly had two or three of everything, from couches to can openers. Not to mention my new husband's T-shirt collection. And his baseball hats. And his coats for every possible weather scenario.

I knew I was in trouble as we were packing up his Calgary house and I sorted through a kitchen drawer, discovering five different bottle openers.

I held them out, saying, "I don't think we need five. Which ones can we toss?"

He paused and looked at them for a very long time before pointing to one. "I guess I could let that one go."

At our new home, kitchen drawers suddenly burst with utensils, closets were stuffed, and we could barely negotiate our way around boxes in the storage room.

And so it was with great joy that I sat my husband down to watch the first episode of the Netflix series *Tidying Up with Marie Kondo*, who has become so celebrated her name is practically a verb. Now, you can "Marie Kondo" your house.

To be honest, we could only stomach one episode of the Netflix series. Marie is sweet, but the drama-ridden families agonizing over their First World problems induced a few rolling eyeballs on our part. However, I did manage to ease my husband into a clutter-freeing mood. (So sexy!)

Although much maligned in some quarters, Marie Kondo offers some good ideas. The clothes in my bedroom drawers were now rolled (rather than folded and stacked), allowing me to actually see everything at once. I delivered five bags of excess clothing and household items to charity; filled our recycling bins several times over (mostly paper—why was I saving all those files?), and tossed a bag or two of garbage.

For those who don't know the KonMari method, it involves holding items and determining whether or not they bring joy to your life. I'm not much for "things," so this was easy. My issue is sentimentality. Tucked away in a storage bin, I still have my daughters' swim team gear. Since swim team was part of their lives more than a dozen years ago, and they're adults now, those caps and goggles aren't going to make it past their foreheads. But *what if* someday I have grandchildren, and they want to do swim team?

You're right, Marie, that bin has to go.

I also have a bin full of my daughters' special sports T-shirts, saved with some vague idea I'd use them to make quilts and present them as high school grad gifts. I can't sew, and they graduated from high school over a decade ago. *Yes, I hear you, Marie.*

The immediate benefit for me as we began Marie-Kondoing our house (there's the verb!) was eliminating clothing. And now that I'm able to see all my clothes at once, I'm actually wearing a wider variety of things.

Bruce's Marie-Kondoing moved a little slower as he battled internal conflicts, considering each item for a *very* long time. It quickly became clear to me that a Mexico holiday would be a faster path to beating the winter blues.

← SHOP 'TIL YOU DROP? NO. →

Here's an example of me shopping:

It's time for new eyewear, and I'd like something that expresses my personality. Something wild and crazy and "out there." (Ha. This is so *not* my personality.) Maybe some red frames. At the very minimum, I want large frames that mark a defiant departure from my current mousey, wear-only-in-the-dark eyewear.

So I wander into a store and start perching frames upon my nose. In the back of my mind, I'm envisioning all those beautiful, laughing, bespectacled models I see in TV commercials. They look so good in glasses. And so happy! (Then—yikes!—I realize I'm picturing the sashay with which Bruce's second ex-wife donned big, loud glasses. Really?) But I carry on with my mission.

Hmm. Bold frames don't actually suit me. I move toward the wire frame section, and then, better, the frameless glasses.

Eventually, I realize I'm not beaming like those models; I don't like wearing glasses. I even consider that perhaps the ex-wife is an ex *because of* her annoyingly loud eyewear.

I exit the store without buying anything, deciding to stick with contact lenses.

I'm not a shopper.

Inevitably, once I decide what I want to buy, find my way into a store, and even identify something I like—I immediately fret that I'll find something better, less expensive, and more appropriate somewhere else. I get purchasing paralysis.

On the other hand, Bruce is a shopping machine. Once, when we first started dating, I accompanied him into a shoe store, made myself comfortable on a chair, and, with a silent sigh, hunkered down for the wait. He marched over to a shelf, picked up a pair of shoes, tried on his size, and, before I could say, "but what about . . ." he was at the counter and then sauntering out the door, shiny bag in hand.

It was dazzling to behold. Even without my glasses.

"ME TIME"?
← BUILDING A BOUNTIFUL GARDEN →

My first garden flourished in those remarkably uncomplicated, post-university, and pre-baby years. At first I was a reluctant gardener. I had books to read, poetry to write, a nine-to-five job . . . but I wanted to impress the boyfriend, and, eventually, I found the process likable, even rewarding.

Fast-forward thirty years to find that particular thrill buried and dormant. I have to contain my rolling eyes when Bruce looks toward the large grassy area in the backyard and becomes exuberant, sprouting words like "backhoe," "deer-fencing," "big bags of soil and mulch," and "tomato plants."

Fact: we both work long hours and leisure time (aside from the aforementioned and *necessary* hockey watching) is more of a concept than a reality. Fact: I once plucked an entire bed of wildflowers, thinking they were weeds. And, finally, fact: not too long ago, we churned up a piece of lawn, planted herbs and veggies on a thick raised bed of soil, watched the plants grow with the pride of new parents, and then lost the entire bounty to a band of bunnies who managed to slide in under the chicken wire fencing that was supposed to protect the garden from pests. So when Bruce gets all bubbly about it, I agree that gardening is a marvelous notion—however, I haven't gone out and purchased a Rototiller.

Still, come springtime, everyone is thinking "garden," so one year, I set out to write something witty and entertaining about our own gardening efforts. However, our story is more akin to tragedy than comedy, so I sought out our friends Shari and Peter, whose thumbs are so green they glow in the dark. As we dined together one evening, I asked, "Do you have any amusing gardening stories?"

"Well," said Shari. "I once weeded out all the asparagus spears. They looked like weeds." (See! I'm not the only one.)

But judging from Peter's glowering look from across the table, I gathered he didn't find that story particularly amusing.

So I turned to him and said, "Didn't you once have a situation with a bird and—um . . . well, there is no good way to put this—but . . . a bird and your nuts?"

Turns out as he plucked nuts from one of his gazillion almond, hazelnut, and walnut trees, a jay hopped from branch to branch, screeching at him every time he picked a nugget from the tree. Mildly amusing for sure!

Peter and Shari have an amazing garden. Every fall, we remind them of our deep friendship by dropping in a little ore frequently around the time they harvest their most spectacular-tasting pears. In the summer, they are the most popular barbecue guests on the block as they arrive with glorious salads—almost too pretty to eat—made entirely of homegrown vegetables. In spring, they give away massive bouquets of heavenly scented red roses . . . and all year long they seem to be feasting on the bounty of their fruit trees.

I personally wish they lived a little closer because after the Big One hits, that's where we're headed. Once the post-quake barter system emerges, things don't look so positive for Bruce and me. I'm not certain that our combined skills of editing, writing, and deciphering public opinion will be very marketable in a post-apocalyptic world: hence our plan to move in with Peter and Shari.

Our dinner conversation moved to other topics, and later, Shari and I sat with little glasses of their *homemade* blackberry port, chatting about our busy work schedules.

Turns out she only has about one day off every week and her "me" time includes weeding, watering, pruning, planting, and plucking the garden. Hauling soil to and fro. Helping Peter fix the fence. And, of course, learning to distinguish between weeds and asparagus.

Hmm. I confess it's not really my idea of "me" time, and I can only hope that Bruce's sprouting horticultural enthusiasm survives about as long as our aforementioned gardening attempts.

← AMAZING RACERS →

When Bruce and I wed in 2014, we added an unusual toast to our reception's glass-clinking speeches. We toasted our exes—the parents of our children—who were invited to the wedding because we are all still good friends. It's this toast that people still talk about.

I thought of this as I travelled to Milan, Italy, in early March 2018 for the opening of Danica's first big solo art exhibit. It was a nutty trip: twenty-two hours getting there, three-and-a-half nights spent in Milan, and twenty-six hours getting back. Bruce couldn't get away, and Derrick-the-ex suffers severe anxiety around flying . . . so they both bowed out. I ended up travelling with Derrick's partner, my daughters' stepmom, Sandra. Some people may raise their eyebrows at this—but it was perfect.

Turns out, we travelled really well together, and that's not necessarily a common thing. There are many people in the world who I love dearly but with whom I cannot travel. But on this trip, Sandra and I always seemed to reach the same decisions on what to do, where to go, what to eat, and when to sleep. We also have similarly advanced coffee addictions and mutually low alcohol tolerance, so we synced well both morning and night.

And we're of the same mind when it comes to packing. Bruce scoffs at me for being such an eager packer. I make a list, pack early, change the list, unpack, repack! It thrilled me to learn that for this trip to Milan, Sandra had also packed two weeks ahead of time—when the weather forecast had temperatures hovering around 12 to 15 degrees—and (like me) had to start packing again as those predicted temperatures plummeted.

It was freakishly cold in Milan that year; it even snowed. We both had clothes in our bags that never got worn as each day we bundled into the same warmest-arrangement of layers.

Early on in our planning, Sandra and I collectively decided, "Meh, we'll just save funds on accommodations and spend the last night at the airport prior to our 7 AM flight out."

We'd both travelled a lot in our twenties and had frequently slept in airports.

Happily, we both came to our senses and decided to book a fourth night at our Airbnb. Unhappily, we both felt an urgency to get to the airport early, and since we didn't know how long it would take to get there, we booked a taxi for 3 AM. We arrived at the airport at precisely 3:11 AM—and the airport didn't open until 4 AM. (*Ahem*, good thing we hadn't planned to sleep at the airport, arriving at midnight.)

The trip home felt like an episode out of the TV show *The Amazing Race*. (In fact, we agreed, we'd make great contestants—who wouldn't cheer for a team of ex- and current wives?) Our plane sat on the tarmac for three hours in Milan, waiting for snow removal in London, our connecting city. Our late arrival there sent us dashing through the terminal to catch our next flight—this one to Calgary. This flight ended up being delayed as well, prompting an even faster, adrenaline-laced run through the Calgary terminal, this time adding stops to clear customs and security, following a long, winding route to the departure gate.

But the point is, we took it all in stride, had lots of laughs, and, throughout the entire trip, always seemed to be on the same page.

The Amazing Race? Watch out!

← TAMING THE EXTROVERTS →

INTROVERTED? HERE'S HOW TO BE MORE SOCIAL reads the title of an *Oprah Magazine* article I happened upon on social media. "Just once," says a Twitter response, "I'd like to see an article like 'Extroverted? Here are some tips on how to be quiet and reflective.'"

For a special section in *Boulevard*, we asked BC entrepreneurs, "What is your superpower?" It set me musing about superpowers and wondering how powerful I'd feel as an extrovert.

Imagine walking into a room full of people and crushing it—ping-ponging from person to person, giving each the perfect dose of chit-chat (albeit, often shallow), peppered with anecdotes (albeit, often incorrectly recalled) and salted with firm handshakes, and the perfect conversational exit.

Bruce is an extrovert, and I consider him with awe as, first, he's always excited to go to a party; second, he's not ready to leave after half an hour; and, third, he happily mingles amid the throng, seemingly eager to talk to everyone there. My introvert-spawned party goals are to arrive late, leave early, and know exactly where the escape areas lie—back porch, bathroom, and edges of the party where fellow introverts huddle. I've learned to seek out other introverts and embark on deeper—if not slightly awkward—one-on-one conversations. (The longer the better—and it usually is a long conversation because introverts don't know how to gracefully move on.)

But is being an extrovert really a superpower?

Years ago, when Bruce and I lived in Calgary, we attended numerous political functions. Since I was new to the city, and he'd been there for years, I knew no one and pretty much stuck to his side as he made his mingle-and-jive moves.

But soon something emerged. After the event, I'd ask him if he'd heard a certain comment, noted a new pairing, caught a bit of body language. Usually it was no, no, no. Also, it turned out that as he was chatting away to a cluster of people, I'd often fall into a side conversation with someone else in the group (usually another introvert), ultimately discovering all sorts of things unbeknownst to my extroverted husband.

Finally, I found that being an introvert helped me to listen. Extroverts, many of whom like to talk a lot, often chatter away to introverts (who are just thankful to appear engaged in a conversation). And as good interviewers know, if you want to find out something, say very little and chances are the speaker will fill the space with words. This brings to mind a certain interview I conducted in 2008 with a charming extrovert based in Calgary. To say the least, I left the interview extremely pleased with all the information I'd pulled from this man who turned out to be my future husband.

So bring on the introvert superheroes! Perhaps we can teach you extroverts how to be quiet and reflective.

Gifts of Joy

HEARTFELT:
← FINDING MOMENTS TO TREASURE →

On September 14, 2016, Bruce stepped out of his truck at the entranceway to Lady Minto Hospital on Salt Spring Island, collapsed, and went into full cardiac arrest.

A nurse, who happened to be leaving at the end of her shift, dropped to her knees to perform CPR. Paddles on a nearby crash cart were rushed into action. Bruce was stabilized and helicoptered to the cardiac care unit at Royal Jubilee Hospital in Victoria, where, within a couple of hours, he had two stents inserted into his heart.

Three days later, he went home—one of only a very small percentage of people to survive this particular type of heart attack, also known as "the widow-maker."

That's the bones of the story. There's a lot of flesh to it as well.

Bruce's family has no history of heart disease. He was an average-weight, non-smoking fifty-six-year-old who, despite a fondness for beer and burgers, ate fairly well and exercised a couple of times a week. The heart attack hit on the blind side.

Several months later, lifestyle changes were in place. We were eating even better, drinking less, and exercising more regularly. (No longer able to consider french fries a food group, our hearts were a little broken as well.)

But the real "flesh" of the story is what an incident like this does to the way you view the world. Clichés abound—"seize the day," "stop and smell the roses," "enjoy life to the fullest." But they are just words until you are forced to look directly into the eye of your own mortality.

A lot of fear follows an event like this. For me, there were haunting images of what might have been—what if it had occurred at home and not the hospital?—and separation angst: Will he have another heart attack while I'm gone?

Eventually time passes, diagnostic tests show excellent results, the cardiologist says the prognosis is good, and the acute anxiety fades. But you realize you've "dodged a bullet" (back to the clichés), and you try to make sense of it all. How do you "live each moment like there is no tomorrow"—now that you really understand there may not be a tomorrow?

And this is the real meat (tofu or salmon, these days) of the story—the question that everyone needs to consider: What are the good, true, honest, and joyful things in your life that make you want to get up in the morning? What drags you down? How can you bring passion, light, and love into your days, and weed out the dissonance?

There are no guidelines to what should or should not make you feel good—it could be an explosion of colour, a thought-provoking painting, or a slice of sweet citrus.

But it's these moments that we need to treasure, and treasure them like there really is no tomorrow.

As we walked a rugged 12-kilometre trail on Malcolm Island—located off the north end of Vancouver Island—I couldn't help but recall the last time we traversed this path.

It was eight years ago, well before we began a regular hiking regime that has significantly increased our fitness level. The hike was one of those instances where the mind goes one way and the body goes the other. We'd set out on the trail amid loose conversations around hiking part of the North Coast Trail to Cape Scott—a significant trek that takes eight hours each way. (These conversations often start with great enthusiasm but falter as we try to envision carrying a case of beer on our backs.) At any rate, about thirty minutes into the first Malcom Island hike, we'd huffed and puffed in agreement that we might not be ready for an eight-hour hike.

This year, the hike was still tough—especially where the path merged into several-storeys-worth of crumbling stairs down and then up ... and then disappearing altogether—but with our newly toned walking muscles, it was much more accessible.

It got me thinking about other times the mind says "Yes!" but the body says "Are you kidding?" This happened to me a couple of times when called upon to participate in parents' teams during my daughters' years of playing sports. Trotting along at half speed on a soccer field, for example, my mind took me sprinting up the wing with the ball, deking out a defender, and placing the ball right in front of the net for a striker to put between the posts. My body? It continued trotting at half speed.

Or the time I got pulled onto a parents' relay team at a swim meet and slotted in for the 50-metre freestyle portion.

It didn't help that I discovered a small hole on the backside of my swimsuit just moments before climbing onto the block and bending (in front of a row of timers) into the "set" position. At the buzzer, I blasted forward and sped through the water to the 25-metre mark . . . and slowly died the entire length back.

But as these thoughts are wont to do, my mind turned to my husband—always fodder for a good yarn—and the time we sat at a bar with a couple of men our age and a couple of younger bucks. The talked turned to rugby, and Bruce confided that, yes, he'd once been a rugby player, too! As pints of beer clinked enthusiastically around the table, a game was planned for the following day.

"When exactly did you play rugby?" I asked innocently as we made our way home.

"High school!" he answered. "I played wing because I was light and fast!"

"And how old are you now?" I wondered aloud as I did the math. "Oh, so that was close to forty years ago. Hmm. Played any rugby since?" I already knew the answer to that one.

Sure enough, the men all turned out, and the game got underway. Five minutes into it, Bruce catches the ball. He sees an opening and charges forward, accelerating across the field to cheers on the sideline . . . but then, like a car of out gas, he starts to decelerate and finally limps off the field. Oh dear. Have you ever seen what a torn hamstring looks like? Purple bruising, from leg top to bottom. Ever seen what a bruised ego looks like?

No matter, the hamstring healed, as did the ego. But there is no rugby or soccer or swim meet in our future. We'll stick to hiking. (Now. How *do* you carry a case of beer on your back?)

Amid fall's glorious colours, weather that's crisp but still infused with warmth, and schedules wonderfully freed up from the chaos of summer, comes an annual tradition on Salt Spring Island: that of the fall fair.

This is a time when the crafty shine. The artistry of quilters hangs like beaming beacons of talent on the walls; handwoven baskets arise in astounding shapes and colours; weavers spin deft demonstrations; pie makers, woodworkers, wine, and beer crafters all emerge from their studios, kitchens, basements, and workshops to proudly display the results of all this know-how and can-do.

In the gardening section, bouquets of flowers bloom in little glass jars as testament to the prowess of wily gardeners—islanders who have somehow outwitted deer, rabbits, weeds, and lack of rainfall to present these glorious vessels of colour.

It's all a little confounding for those of us who struggle to thread a needle or grow a tomato. Both my daughters are artists and as children they thrived at the fall fair, amassing ribbons and trophies, while I eyed my pantry and wondered if I could make a packaged cake appear homemade.

Although Bruce is a talented musician and—sigh—able to paint a lovely watercolour, we're at the same level when it comes to gardening, baking, woodworking, et cetera. That would be the basement level. Our gardening efforts have literally gone to the deer, and so now we console ourselves by finding enjoyment in watching these four-legged flower-eaters as they wander about our acreage, shredding the foliage—but generally looking cute.

We have a towering cherry tree in the backyard that produces rich red cherries—if you can get to them before the birds and other creatures. This summer we watched midday as a tribe of raccoons drunkenly made their way from branch to branch stuffing their cheeks with cherries. They were too adorable—a big fat mother and five babies—to shoo away. Later, we saw a deer standing on her hind legs to get at cherries on the lower branches, birds flapping about in the tree's upper foliage, and a rabbit at the base of the trunk nibbling on anything left behind. There would be no bowl of cherries at the fall fair with our names neatly attached to it. (If only we could move the tree itself. It would surely win a prize!)

We also have a gorgeous grapevine that has, over the years, been our most successful gardening attempt (really, the only successful one, and—truth be told—we didn't actually plant it). It produces clusters of creamy purple champagne grapes that practically melt on the tongue. This year we sampled a few and said, "So close! We'll pick them tomorrow." And the very next day, the entire vine was wiped clean. There'd be none of our grapes at the fall fair either.

But things did look a little different this year on the talent landscape, since Julian, our man-of-all-trades friend, had taught my husband a few handyman tricks. It was quite charming to see Bruce—previously more comfortable in a suit than work clothes—suddenly rolling out the table saw, router, hammer, and nails. His feigned nonchalance belied his glee at his new-found skillset.

Our home needed trim in various places and he was the man to do it, eagerly setting the saw whirring and then hammering, drilling . . . and proudly dragging me (and any visitors who happened by) around the property to show off the results of his handiwork.

So as we drove to the fair this year, I mused, "If only there was a 'trim' section, you almost certainly would have won a ribbon—maybe even a trophy!"

I found this funnier than he did.

But aside from all this, the fall fair is a must-do annual event. In addition to shining a spotlight on everything local—from farm animals to classic cars, grad fundraisers, the launch of political campaigns, and rides for the kids—the fair emerges as a sort of "relationship reset button" for islanders.

After hiding in their homes all summer to avoid the island's hordes of tourists, people are curious. What unlikely couple has paired up in these past few months? Which relationships couldn't take the summer heat?

For those in a new relationship, it's a time to grab your beau's hand and march boldly through the eagerly awaiting crowds. If your new partner suddenly reveals a new direction in sexuality—even better!

It's also a time to keep your wits about you. You *will* see everyone you know, so be prepared to duck into the long line at the Pie Ladies' booth should you wish to avoid your husband's ex. And pick your spots. For example, Bruce and I know we're more likely to find friends in the beer garden than the pet show parade (mostly because it takes place at 8 AM on Sunday). And everyone will be at the Muffin Madness corral; however, there will be no idle chitchat here. Instead, a solemn and hushed atmosphere will ensue as spectators watch and wait for the cow to drop her muffin—hopefully on a square they've purchased.

Ultimately, despite having to suffer through the tidal wave of talent and dodge the odd person here and there, I do love the fall fair for its opportunity to reconnect with friends, listen to homegrown music, and munch on a fair food staple like roasted corn on the cob. Oh, and the pigs. I *love* the pigs.

However. Don't let my fall fair exuberance fool you. I'm beyond the fair now and eyeing the upcoming holiday season. I'm thinking perhaps I can hand craft a few ornaments for the tree.

As I sat in the emergency room at St. Paul's Hospital in Vancouver, the first diagnosis came back: concussion. For at least a week, there would be no reading, writing, iPhone Scrabble, or even complex conversations. Walking any distance was unlikely. But most important . . . I would have to turn off my brain.

Bruce and I burst out laughing. My brain is king. It doesn't turn off. I check off to-do items in my mind as I try to fall asleep. I carry a detailed, colour-coded calendar in my head, not to mention myriad ferry schedules and a steel-trap memory. I am the go-to person in the household for information; Siri can't hold a candle to me. Turn off my brain. Ha.

Good that we were still laughing, though. Hours earlier I had taken a tumble down a flight of stairs at a hotel, first shattering my elbow as I landed on it and then concussing my head as I careened into a concrete wall.

I was still processing life with a concussion when the elbow diagnosis came in. Surgery was scheduled for the next day: the bones would be wired together and a plate and pins attached. I would go home to Salt Spring with a weighty elbow-to-shoulder cast and a complex-looking sling.

And as it turned out, the cocktail of painkillers over the next week ensured my brain stayed safe and cozy and pretty much shut off. And even without the medicine, it just didn't function. It took me a week to focus enough to watch Netflix, ten days to read, and almost two weeks before I could play iPhone Scrabble. I spent the final half hour of an hour-long conference call for work with my head resting on the desk. Afterward, I went straight back to bed.

The fact that turning my brain off was my biggest concern back there in the ER became amusing as, for four weeks, I tried to train my left hand to do the work of the right. Sometimes with a tangle of twisted shirt around my neck and arms—trying to dress myself—I realized I really should get better at asking for help. Things are tricky with the wrong hand: try brushing your teeth. Heck, try putting toothpaste on your toothbrush. Try using your wrong hand on a mouse or mouse pad.

And computer dictation—which I used to craft work emails and texts—wasn't much faster.

So as life that summer slowed down, I searched for the life lesson. I realized that during those four weeks, when I found myself frustrated by the amount of time it took to do something, I learned to breathe in and say, "But what does it matter? The one thing I have right now is time." And so I slowly navigated my computer using dictation and my left hand; I emptied the dishwasher one item by one item; I painstakingly cleared my dinner plate with a left-hand-held fork; I even folded laundry . . . at a snail's pace. Instead of creating long to-do lists every day, I set smaller goals.

And slowly, things changed—maybe even for the better. Instead of rolling out of bed and going straight to my home office computer on those glorious summer days, I sipped my morning coffee outside with bare feet planted on the earth, revelling in the glorious scenery around me.

Ironically, as I considered the lesson of "slowing down," I realized I took that fateful staircase because I was impatient. It was an older building, and the elevator was slow. The stairs would be faster . . . a better use of my time. (Hmm.)

As things meshed back to "normal" that autumn, I looked forward to having a full-firing brain and full use of my "bionic" right elbow, now held together with a plate and several screws.

But I also hoped to take my lesson to heart. I hoped I would remember to slow down and savour the season.

← GIFTS OF JOY →

Back in the early 2000s, my uncle Bill was flipping through TV channels when the Lotto 6/49 numbers flashed on the screen. The numbers looked familiar. In fact, they looked *really* familiar.

Ever since he was a boy choosing sports jerseys, Uncle Bill had picked out numbers heavy in 4s and 1s. He had been using a 4-and-1 combination on lotto tickets for years, but this particular week he asked his wife, Shirley, for her lucky number and inserted 20 for his usual 11.

He waited another fifteen minutes for the numbers to flash on again. Then he went upstairs and said to Shirley, "I think we may have just won a substantial amount of money." They slept with the ticket under their mattress, rose early, and quietly started their journey to the lottery centre in Vancouver to claim their $2.4-million prize.

Amid any seasonal chatter about gifts, I like to think of my uncle's amazing generosity—and the gift of joy he gave to our family. Many of us dream about divvying up the bucks of a big win, but I like what my uncle did with his winnings, and not only because a nice sum came my way.

Immediately upon collecting the cheque, he walked into several banks and paid off the mortgages of his three children, who were all in their thirties. He gave them a little fun money, but the bulk of their gains will come from the money he invested, which they will inherit. For himself . . . not so much. He bought a few things, like a new set of golf clubs.

GIFTS OF JOY 163

But a big chunk of it he handed out at a huge family gathering to people I'd become accustomed to seeing only at funerals. This was a much more joyous occasion! None of us had any idea how much our cheques would be, and most were dumbstruck by the number of zeros. (In a wicked older sibling moment, I looked at my brother's cheque—which matched mine precisely—and said, "Yikes, you only got that much?") Uncle Bill also slipped ten thousand dollars to the clerk who sold him the ticket.

In the years since, Uncle Bill and Shirley have travelled the world. They live comfortably but not ostentatiously. In my home, I have an "Uncle Bill bathroom," built with the gift he gave me.

Years later, with his health failing, Bill decided to spread the love again, renting a food- and booze-laden box suite at Rogers Arena and bringing eighteen members of our hockey-crazy family to a Vancouver Canucks game. It was fantastic to once again join with family and share an experience, and a good reminder of what any holiday season is all about: family, friends, sharing time together. It was another gift of joy.

Back at Rogers Arena, as we gathered our coats at the end of the evening, my uncle declared it had been the best night of his life. And somehow that sums it all up right there. Sharing time with his family trumped that night more than fifteen years earlier when he saw those winning numbers flash on the screen.

← DREAMING OF A "GREEN" CHRISTMAS →

After thirty years of holiday-season column writing—often for multiple publications—I realized one year that the well of Christmas creativity was running dry. I'd pulled anecdotes from every holiday season I could remember. I'd gone serious; I'd gone humorous. To gift or not to gift? Christmas with a holiday humbug husband; Christmas with a festive, fanatic husband. I've written about the true meaning of the season (I've come up with several different "true meanings"), and I've attended myriad holiday events, all seeking fodder for my Christmas columns.

So one year, as I struggled to find a unique holiday theme, my mind settled on a recent media trip to Jamaica, which had occurred just weeks after the legalization of marijuana in Canada. On the trip, the two of us Canadians were regarded with a new aura of respect, tinged with envy at our country's progressive attitude. And how ironic, everyone noted, to be sitting in the "ganja" capital of the world, where recreational pot use was still illegal.

Early one morning in Jamaica, I stumbled bleary-eyed out of my room (pre-coffee, so you can picture that) and saw a fellow beckoning to me from the beach. Without my glasses (or coffee!), I mistakenly recognized him as one of the small media tour group, and trotted toward him.

"Wanna buy some ganja?" he asked.

Two weeks earlier, I might have gulped and said, "No, thanks," and scuttled away. Now, however, I could toss my head and give a little laugh. "Dude, I'm from Canada. I don't need to buy ganja on the beaches of Jamaica."

What does this have to do with Christmas, you ask? Well, that year, in an effort to find a unique column theme, I wondered if I could write something humourous about how the legalization of pot might change up the season for some. So I did a little Internet research.

First, I found seasonal edibles. "Dreaming of a Green Christmas?" one pot website asked. "Here are 11 cannabis recipes for the holidays." Recipes followed for holiday essentials such as Smashed & Roasted Red Potatoes with Herbs & Cannabis, Cream of Cannabis Soup, Ganja-Glazed Nuts, Cannabis Gravy, and Ganjabread House.

I also found the expected hand-wringing and angst: "It's December 2018, and you're responsible for organizing your office Christmas party," wrote one newspaper. "You've got the food, you've got the booze. Should you also buy a few joints or edibles now that marijuana is legal in Canada?"

Here are some other headlines I found: WHAT I LEARNED FROM MY CHRISTMAS EDIBLES NIGHTMARE, 21 COMPELLING REASONS WHY YOU SHOULD SMOKE WEED ON CHRISTMAS (most were not compelling at all), 15 WAYS WEED CAN MAKE CHRISTMAS BETTER (pretty sure the writer was high when writing this one), and the intriguing WHICH IS CHEAPER: WALMART'S 'WEED CHRISTMAS TREE' OR ACTUAL WEED?

I also found "green" gifts—like the Let's Get Baked T-shirt— and some very exciting YouTube videos with titles, such as "Girl gets boyfriend pound of weed for Christmas."

So I crafted it all into a column, chortling as I wrote it, thrilled I had a new holiday angle. Ready to submit it, I started thinking about the publication's demographic, which, I realized, was heavy on seniors. *No matter*, I thought, *I'll run it past a couple of women in their seventies.*

So what did they think? Funny, right?

It didn't help that in my rough draft, there was a typo in the first refernce of the word "ganja." One woman wrote back, saying, "At first I couldn't figure out what you were talking about because I didn't know that ganja was a term for marijuana. I looked up 'the ganga capital of the world' only to discover that it is the river Ganges, hence my confusion."

Oh dear.

Neither woman took offence at the column, but the second one added, "I think it's a bit sad that it's such a big deal."

Sad? Confusing? So much for my sense of humour. I sighed, filed the column away, and cobbled together a string of memories around gift-giving.

← OUT OF THE WOODS →

Good times and bad times—all in one day. It was the best afternoon ever at our favourite local bar, Moby's Pub. But the windstorm of December 20, 2018, was as close to a natural disaster as you can get on Salt Spring Island.

Working in my home office earlier that day, I barely noticed the wind until suddenly a crack and a crash coincided with the power going out. Losing power isn't unusual in a windstorm on Salt Spring. But it was unexpected when the gusts upended a tree, which narrowly missed the barbecue in our front yard and crushed an outdoor table. Bruce and I ran outside, shocked at the force of the gusts. As we surveyed the damage in the front yard, two trees came slamming down near the driveway, one brushing the side of a truck, the other landing on an outbuilding. Our friend Julian, who lives with us from time to time, had to jump out of the way.

In fact, all hell was breaking loose on our property and the road above it. Branches fell like rain, and cracks and thuds reverberated through the forest. Bruce and Julian grabbed chainsaws and set out to cut a tree blocking our neighbour's driveway. Danica (home for the Christmas holidays) and I walked over with them. We were stunned to see a massive tree tangled in broken wires and hanging precariously across the road, with vehicles trying to drive under it. After Bruce and Julian cleared the neighbour's driveway and moved on to cutting the tree across the roadway (luckily the wires were all dead at this point), a primal journalistic instinct kicked in, and I said to Danica, who had grown up in a news-chasing home, "We need to get photos!"

And so we set off. The wind was blowing hard, but it wasn't a steady force. Still, it was the gusts that shocked us. We quickly realized being out in this storm was a bad idea and turned back, but as the wind revved up with fury, we heard cracks in three directions around us. Not knowing where the branches and trees were falling, we dove into a bus shelter, hearts hammering. Then we ran for home!

By mid-afternoon, the windstorm seemed to have abated slightly, and Julian, still unnerved by the close call with the falling fir, was ready to hit the pub. We had no power to cook a late lunch, and we all agreed we were thirsty!

Danica, who was working by kerosene lamplight on a drawing, decided to stay back. So the three of us jumped into the truck, dodged fallen branches on the road, and headed into town. At Moby's, a disaster-prompted joviality reigned. With the power out, the bar served bottled beer instead of draft and switched its food menu to sandwiches only. The wind continued to blow outside, a huge limb landed on a car in the parking lot, and we watched a rowboat make a dramatic exit from a vessel in the harbour as the windows rattled ominously beside us. Darkness fell; candles were lit. Eventually, Dale, the manager, announced "last call" because it was too dark inside the pub to be safe. About twenty people remained . . . and, all at once, the whole crew started singing Christmas carols—a magical moment of Yuletide spirit. And then it was time to leave.

The first inkling that the wind hadn't abated during our bar stint, but had, in fact, wound up faster and harder, was the lineup of cars on the main road, stuck and unable to get by a huge mess of fallen trees further up the highway. We managed to pass the line by driving on the wrong side of the road to get to our turn-off—where we discovered a natural disaster in the making. Our street was unrecognizable. We drove under trees hanging across wires and around mountains of debris. At the top of our driveway, it looked like a bomb had exploded. People with chainsaws, illuminated by headlights, were trying to make the road passable, but all I could think of was Danica, sitting in the house at the bottom of the driveway, all alone. And who knew what the house looked like!

Motherly fear clutched my heart, and I practically fell out of the truck, diving under the trees on the road to get to the driveway, now a jumbled mess of foliage. I had to crawl under and over thick tree trunks and through tangles of branches, scraping my legs and arms, but propelled by a mother-fear-fueled near-hysteria.

Finally, I shot through the front door, shouting "Danica!" as I stumbled into the kitchen. And there she was, drawing away by candlelight, headphones on, humming along to the music. She looked up.

"What?" she asked.

The next morning, our five acres looked apocalyptic. We had twenty trees down, including six across the driveway, plus one massive fir uprooted and hanging in the trees, luckily facing away from the house. The road at the top of our driveway looked like a war zone, with wires dangling everywhere, a transformer smashed on the pavement, trees down, and a hydro pole sheared in half.

For someone who's hugged a tree or two, the devastation was heartbreaking. We lost a grand old, moss-covered maple tree and a one-hundred-year-old cedar, as well as firs and alders. And the appearance of our property's forest changed dramatically.

The four of us packed into the truck, luckily parked at the top of the driveway (if we hadn't gone to the bar, we would have had to cut through all those trees on the driveway simply to get a vehicle out) and took a tour around the island. Bruce and Julian packed chainsaws, just in case. We called it "disaster-tourism," and indeed, the island was devastated, with many areas completely inaccessible. Had I still been at the newspaper, I would have considered any one of the dozens of scenes we witnessed as worthy of a front-page photo.

Later, back at the house, we started the cleanup. But really, our adventure had just begun because within days, everyone else arrived home for Christmas . . .

WHAT WE DID ON
← OUR CHRISTMAS VACATION →

I have about thirty years' worth of Christmas dinner photos. You probably have them, too. They all look much the same: there's the red and green candles flickering beside a holiday-patterned platter of turkey, bowls of steaming vegetables, and mashed potatoes. There's the gravy boat and matching plates holding cranberry sauce and gherkin pickles, the once-a-year china, gleaming silverware, and place settings topped with Christmas crackers. A fairly regular cast of nicely dressed people sits at the table, most wearing grimace-smiles that say "pleeease get on with the photo so we can eat."

But among my collection of photos, 2018's version stands out. The candles are there, yes, but the dining room table has moved, the cast is not dressed in any finery, and the dinner feast is markedly unfestive. The faces, illuminated only by candlelight, seem a bit weary. The clothes are bulky; two people are wearing toques. The red-and-green-checked tablecloth is there, and the crackers and the wine, but I'm not seeing the fancy dinnerware, and, instead of holding a traditional holiday spread, the plates are topped with burgers.

In this year, just five days before Christmas, hurricane force winds blew a wild twist into our traditional holiday season. A smashed transformer, a severed hydro pole, debris, and a twist of downed power lines at the top of the driveway said it all: there would be no power for days (eight days, to be exact).

We had eight people at home for the holidays: our four kids—thankfully, now all in their twenties—plus Sierra's partner, Jon, as well as Julian, Bruce, and me.

At first, we had use of a small generator and chose to power the fridge for a few hours at a time. We lit the house at night with candles—over sixty of them during the next eight days—and called into use a couple of propane lanterns, pulled from our camping gear. Luckily, we have a three-burner gas cookstove and a barbecue, so we organized a cook station on the back deck.

We also have an emergency kit, finally purchased just a few months prior to the windstorm. Bruce pulled out the kit's headlamp and wore it with great enthusiasm—a one-eyed monster roaming the dark, inside and out.

Our existence shifted to pioneer mode. With only about six hours of daylight, there was much to do! We sawed and bucked up the trees on the driveway and cleared some of the debris in the yard, building a massive bonfire one afternoon. In the kitchen, we chopped vegetables and prepped food to cook after dark.

A boil water advisory was issued immediately following the storm, but on the third day, the rush of water from the taps slowed to a trickle and then stopped completely. Now daylight meant filling buckets with water from a rain barrel to use for dishwashing and toilet flushing, and to boil for brushing our teeth and face washing. Eventually, we lost the battle of powering the fridge and moved the food into outdoor bins, realizing this meant we'd lose all of our freezer food.

In the evenings we lived in the living room, huddled around the wood stove. Bedding, extra blankets, chairs, and even the dining room table followed us into the space. We hunkered down, sipped wine, munched on simple meals, chatted, and paired off to play Scrabble or cribbage (but never moving too far from the stove).

It was cold—especially at night. Four people could sleep near the wood stove, but Bruce and I retreated to our bedroom to sleep and Julian went to his. Danica tucked into her child-hood room, which was probably the coldest of the three. She slept under two blankets and wore four layers of clothing— a silk shirt, merino wool sweater, cashmere sweater, and down jacket. She wrapped a vest around her face. Similarly, I wore a Lululemon ski shirt that became a second skin for the entire week. We all tucked into our warmest layers, wearing them day and night.

The tree—traditionally decorated on Christmas Eve— remained undressed in the corner, a sad string of unlit lights draped over its boughs. But on Christmas night, we used the last bit of gasoline (fuel stations on the island had run out) in the generator to turn on that string of lights. It felt a bit like a Christmas miracle.

For days, we'd held on to the plan of serving a traditional Christmas dinner, with Bruce and Julian theorizing on the best way to cook a turkey on the barbecue. But when the water stopped on December 23, it all just suddenly seemed like too much. So we cooked burgers—vegetarian and turkey—and placed them on paper plates. We played games at the table by candlelight and drank through our (happily well-stocked) liquor cabinet.

After it was all over, the kids mused, "How will we ever beat that Christmas?"

At times like these, the world becomes a lot smaller, and the things that are important become bigger. I learned that all the holiday trimmings—the tree, the turkey dinner, the gifts— are small things. Huddling in front of the wood stove with the people you love is a big thing. In fact, for that week, it meant everything.

So, despite the hardship we endured, I look with fondness upon 2018's un-festive Christmas dinner photograph, and it will continue to be a standout in my collection.

← THE MATTER OF THE PINK SHIRT →

Over the last few years, my younger daughter and I have embarked on a strange path of "giving." It began when Sierra received a flowery pink flannel shirt from a well-meaning but fashion-challenged friend. She immediately gave it to me; I gave it back. Then we started getting creative.

I stuffed it into a boot for her to find in the winter. I found it in my closet, hidden under another shirt on a hanger. I popped it into the glovebox of her car. She had it delivered by a third party as a birthday gift. (That third party happened to be John Bateman, son of famed Canadian artist Robert Bateman. For just an instant, as John handed me the "gift," I thought, *It's a Bateman original!)*

This pattern of one-upmanship also played out years ago between my father and I when he was still alive. For example, when I crushed my finger in a window and my fingernail fell off, I took the blackened nail, put it in an envelope, and mailed it to my dad, without any accompanying letter.

Then, when Danica was a baby, I took to leaving small reminders of our presence whenever I visited. I'd take one of her diapers—disposable for travelling—wrap it in a plastic bag and leave it in places for my Dad to find, like wrapped up in his pyjamas. Again, nothing was said, and I grew ever more creative and gleeful.

Then I started to notice a smell in my car. Without thinking much of it, I cleared out some of the baby gear, and a few days later made a tentative search for rotting food under the seat. But the smell persisted; in fact, it worsened. Finally, I took the car's entire interior apart, crawling under the bucket seats, even pulling out the bench in the back. I scoured the trunk. I scrubbed the upholstery. Nothing.

Eventually the problem was discovered under the hood: my father had carefully attached a fish head to the underside of the motor, where it happily rotted. My offences against him were subsequently subdued.

But back to the pink shirt. For a long time, I thought my most recent prank would be impossible to beat. I started by creating an official-looking letter that appeared to come from a modelling agency that Sierra had worked for periodically. I went online, downloaded the agency's logo, and placed it along the top of a piece of paper as letterhead. Then I typed in an official-looking font:

Dear Sierra Lundy,
The Numa Network is pleased to announce forthcoming
compliance with the Government of Canada's newly

created Strategic Model Management requirements
as set out on June 15, 2018, by the Ministry of Public
Expression.

To this end, we are asking that as of July 1, 2018,
each model and actor in the Numa Network include
the contents of the attached package at all shoots and
interviews.

Neglecting to include these items will put our mod-
els in a non-compliance position, so this requirement is
non-negotiable.

Thank you for you cooperation. We are proud to
include you in the Numa Network team!

I placed the pink shirt in a brown envelope, stapled the letter to it, and dropped it into a larger bubble-wrapped envelope. I created a label with the agency logo, placed it and some stamps on the outer envelope, and then drew in a postmark before sneaking it into her mailbox. I could hardly contain myself for the next few days—and she fell for it completely! I was thrilled with my cleverness.

And then, months, even a year went by, and the pink shirt was forgotten. I was watching TV one evening as Bruce and his band practised in an outbuilding elsewhere on the property. Hungry, I started rummaging through the freezer and finally pulled out a loaf of gluten-free bread that had been frozen for a while. As I cut into it, I realized something was horribly amiss. It had been hollowed out and inside sat a cylinder-shaped package, wrapped in plastic. I was absolutely horrified—certain, somehow, I'd stumbled onto a drug-smuggling operation. Where did I buy the bread? Could the local grocery store be involved in smuggling? What if someone finds out we have his heroin in our freezer!

I shoved the bread back in the freezer, returned to the living room, and sent a text to Bruce, expressing alarm over the situation with the bread in the freezer. Bruce, who, it turned out, was in on the joke, asked that I take a closer look and to please let him know what exactly had been hidden in the bread.

Okay. You can guess the rest of story. Needless to say, Sierra was beyond gleeful, especially when I told her that I'd been sitting on the couch, Googling "smuggling in bread."

← GETAWAY ON MOTHER'S DAY →

My adult daughters and I have embarked on a tradition of stealing away on one-night surprise getaways, once or twice a year when we are all in the same city. I carefully guard the secret destination while they attempt to trip me up on providing details, and then I whisk them away to places unknown.

The excursions usually involve lounging in a hot tub or warm-water pool, consuming a bottle (or more) of wine, and sharing lots of information. (This sometimes borders on "too much information." Does a mother really need to know all this?)

With Mother's Day in mind one year, I created a journey with a bit of a spin, aiming to evoke some cherished memories, while creating some new ones. I dropped random hints, with which they somehow concluded we were renting electric bikes and brought along their helmets. (If this were a text message, I'd insert the shrugging emoji here).

Our trip began at Victoria's buffet-style Green Cuisine restaurant, which is central to our family mythology. Derrick and I were regulars in the early '90s, when it first opened.

Our daughters subsequently embraced it, and, over the years, meals here became a "test" for all prospective suitors—both mine, after my divorce, and the girls' boyfriends. If a boy liked Green Cuisine, he passed. If not . . . well, he could expect a "Dear John" email. (Later, other boy tests emerged. For example, texts that confused there/their/they're or your/you're usually rendered the texter as nixed.) And as a side note, Bruce, who was an Alberta meat lover when we met, barely passed the restaurant test; however, now a west coaster, he happily obliges our green cuisine. And his grammar is excellent.

Packed into the car—a familiar place for the three of us—we headed up Vancouver Island. For our second stop, I wanted to introduce my artist daughters to famed artist and master-storyteller Arthur Vickers, who—among the hundreds of people I've interviewed over the years—remains one of my very favourites. At his gallery in Cowichan Bay, Arthur often waits to see if one of his pieces resonates with a viewer. If it does, he tells the story behind it. We were blessed with three stories, including one that brought tears to all of our eyes. The best stories are the ones that move you.

From soul-touching to body-warming, our next stop was at a winery for a tasting. I wish I could think of another, more meaningful reason, but basically it was because . . . we like drinking wine. Next, we hit up a favourite up-island restaurant to acquire a feast-to-go and headed to our destination: (surprise!) Tigh-Na-Mara Resort in Parksville.

I chose the resort for several reasons: first, the spa's mineral pool provided the requisite soothing water in which to float about and share too much information; second, the lounge in the restaurant offered up the important glasses of wine (more information). But most important, the resort sits at the edge of Rathtrevor Beach. And on a sandy walk the next morning, we watched the tide roll in and dined on memories of this place, which was a huge part of all of our childhoods. Even my mom as a child played in the sand at this beach, where the tide goes out further than the eye can see and then slowly rolls in over the hot sand. Black-and-white photos from my childhood show my brother and I immersed in buckets and shovels and sandcastle-building; while pictures taken years later, now in colour, show little Danica and Sierra also dashing about in the surf. Derrick and I walked here in the pre-baby years; Bruce and I now revel in its beauty in the empty-nest years.

Later the same day, we motored back over the Malahat, met up with Nana in Victoria, and embarked on an afternoon of three-generational, mother-daughter pampering at the Oak Bay Beach Hotel. Although this hotel has been rebuilt several times over the last century and now rises majestically on the Oak Bay waterfront, it has, in its various incarnations, been a part of our family's history. Sifting through my own memories, I see myself dressed in my Sunday best—frills and black patent shoes—attending lunchtime smorgasbords with my grandparents at the hotel's dining room, and later, drinking one of my first cocktails at the hotel's famous Snug Pub. Our connection to the old hotel goes even further back because my paternal grandfather was a construction foreman during its post-fire reconstruction in the 1930s. For years, my family kept architectural drawings of the hotel rolled up in long tubes in the basement.

So on this day, with another nod to family, there was more floating about in mineral pools, followed by pedicures for two and manicures for two. Danica and I felt slightly smug as we chose the pedicures and got to lounge in huge, comfy reclining seats with ocean views for our pampering. But then the manicure twosome got to flash their nails about for the rest of the day while our pedicures disappeared into socks.

While all our getaway excursions have been memorable and a testament to the closeness that remains between the three of us, as well as my mom, the fact that this trip was created for Mother's Day and had a family theme made it even more special. For, above and beyond anything else in my life, being a mother has been the most wonderful, significant, and rewarding experience I have ever had.

← AND ONTO THE NEXT CHAPTER →

As I write this final chapter, it has been three decades since Gail and I sat in Moby's Pub, envisioning the possibilities of a world in which we were mothers. It seems like yesterday, but I could never have imagined all the intricate twists and turns of this journey.

There are a few reasons this is the right place to stop and type the final sentences.

It finishes with Mother's Day, and motherhood is one of the threads that ties all these words together.

The moment I became a mother, I realized this was the most important, rewarding, interesting, all-consuming job I could ever want. There's a depth of love here that can't be described. And an understanding that my life is no longer the centre of my universe. My children are more important to me than me. And I have had the most blessed life with my daughters.

Indeed, this collection finishes as my daughters settle into their own worlds: Danica as a visual artist, living in New York City with her husband Tim; Sierra as a (fashion-forward) singer-songwriter living in Victoria. Our lives remain wonderfully interwoven. We text every day. Danica and I chat often via FaceTime; Sierra and I visit frequently. I'm still called on to be a mother—and a friend. I also have the joy of being a stepmom to Dylan, who lives not too far from Danica in New York City, and Jade, who is in Vancouver.

With my work based in Victoria where my mom lives, I visit and stay with her often. (And we text constantly during hockey games—especially when the Canucks are winning. If they're losing, the texting generally stops: we don't want to talk about it.) Derrick and Sandra are still a part of our lives, as is Susan, Dylan and Jade's mom. And I remain close with both Shari and Kai.

My friendship with Gail remains. Although our paths have diverged at times, they always seem to merge again just down the way. It is a huge gift to have a friend who has walked the decades beside you, as a witness to your life, an enduring confidante, and someone who holds a share of your memories. Over the years, Gail and I have literally experienced all of life together, from the birth of her daughter Chloe to the death of her husband Michael.

Now also marks the perfect place to type the final words in this book because it is spring 2020, and our whole world has changed. The COVID-19 pandemic has altered our lives in irreversible ways. It is a pivotal time.

And this brings me to Bruce, the man who has brought so much joy to the second part of my life. For the last several months, Bruce and I have lived together in COVID-mandated isolation. Unlike many, we are lucky to have a house and acreage in which to spread out. But it doesn't matter. We could live together in a box and never tire of each other's company. When Bruce and I wed, we had a traditional 'Namgis carver create our wedding bands. Mine depicts an eagle; Bruce's is a whale. Together, we realized, we are grounded and yet have wings. During these last few months, our relationship has flourished, blooming like the glorious spring around us.

We have become epic walkers, trading in our sports-watching evenings for daily walks that last anywhere from one to three hours. We've discovered new trails by setting out on less-clearly marked paths, unsure of where we're going but ultimately finding spectacular new spots. Our conversations weave together, touching on our many shared passions, and then disentangle, as for a while, our steps are taken in compatible silence. And because of these walks, we've had a front-row seat to an intimate unfolding of spring. We've watched the glory of the landscape transforming, bursting, and presenting itself as a living piece of art in lush, vivid colour.

It has struck me at certain times—like when I finish my day's work hours earlier than in the "olden days," or when I dig about in my cute little rock garden—that there will come a point when we look back upon these months and, despite the hardships, will recognize them as "good times."

I can't help but think of our wedding vows: *Bruce, you are my best friend ... You are a sunrise bursting in colour, like the promise of a new day unfolding. You are the heartbeat beside me as we walk side by side, hand in hand. Today, I give you my heart. I promise to laugh with you, cry with you, and grow old with you.*

And so it goes.

Acknowledgements

The strength of a good book comes down to its characters, and I was given a wealth of them. First and foremost, thank you to the many family members mentioned in these pages—you've provided much fodder for my weird sense of humour and have, over the years, gracefully accepted my gentle-but-rather-public teasing. So thank you to my daughters, Danica Lundy and Sierra Lundy; my husband, Bruce Cameron; my parents, Barbara and the late Douglas Dicker, and my brother, Craig Douglas; my stepkids, Dylan Cameron and Jade Cameron, and their mom, Susan Harris; my ex-husband, Derrick Lundy, and his partner Sandra Smith; my wonderfully generous aunt and uncle, Bill and Shirley Gosling; and others in the Cameron clan: Craig Cameron, Sandra Odendahl, Jim Cameron, Sharon Cameron, Cameron Pratt, and the late Lorna Cameron.

Thank you also to all these wonderful women, most of whom are named in this book, and who share a host of memories with me: Gail Sjuberg, Shari Macdonald, Sandy Buyze-Morgan, the late Sandy Consiglio, Kai Fishleigh, Grace Morgan, Chloe Sjuberg, Prairie Moat, Cecile Petra, Frances Deas, Sue Spencer, Jessica Grace, Mikaela Morgan, Christine Mauro, Sarah Lundy, Heidi Adhofer,

Lia Crowe, and, of course, Blythe Danner. Thanks to the boys in the book: Derek Lundy, Julian Low, Peter McFarlane, John Bateman, Jon Middleton, Tim Spellman, Carson Isenor, Dylan Lundy, Arthur Vickers, Stefan Heine, Al Janusas, and Mark LeCorre.

Thank you, Bruce, Danica, Sierra, and my mom, for reading a first draft, making invaluable suggestions, and not asking me to take out any compromising information, and to Gail, who also read a first draft and did a most helpful first edit.

Thank you also to Tony Richards and Joyce Carlson, who were publishers at the *Gulf Islands Driftwood* all those years ago when my first columns appeared; and to Penny Sakamoto and Black Press Media for printing a more recent series of my family columns; as well as my publishers at *Boulevard*, *Tweed*, and *Pearl* magazines: Mario Gedicke, Janet Gairdner, and Dale Naftel.

To all the great at people at Heritage House Publishing, specifically Lara Kordic, Nandini Thaker, Jacqui Thomas, and editor Paula Marchese: thank you so much for taking on this project with such skill and enthusiasm and making it all the better.

Thanks to my favourite musicians for the soundtrack to the last few years, Sierra's band, Ocie Elliott, and Bruce's bands, Everyday People and Swamp Donkey; and to Moby's Pub, where it all began—a few times.

LIA CROWE

Susan J. Lundy has been writing stories since she could first hold a pencil. A former journalist, she's currently a freelance writer and managing editor of the *Boulevard* Magazine Group, plus several smaller publications. Born and raised in Victoria, BC, she is a graduate of the University of Victoria's creative writing and journalism programs. She has received numerous writing awards and is a two-time recipient of the prestigious Jack Webster Award. In 2013, her first book, *Heritage Apples: A New Sensation*, was published by Touchwood Editions. Her passion for writing is expressed these days in humour essays, travel stories, and creative non-fiction. She lives on Salt Spring Island with her husband, Bruce Cameron, and their new dog Zorro, and is in frequent contact with her adult children, Danica Lundy, Sierra Lundy, Dylan Cameron, and Jade Cameron.

Discover more laugh-out-loud books from Heritage House

wherever fine books are sold

Grandfathered: Dispatches from the Trenches of Modern Grandparenthood

Ian Haysom

ISBN 978-1-77203-333-5

Hard Knox: Musings from the Edge of Canada

Jack Knox

ISBN 978-1-77203-149-2

Opportunity Knox: Twenty Years of Award-Losing Humour Writing

Jack Knox

ISBN 978-1-77203-208-6

The Survival Guide to British Columbia

Ian Ferguson

ISBN 978-1-77203-284-0

Christmas in Mariposa: Sketches from Canada's Legendary Little Town

Jamie Lamb

ISBN 978-1-77203-287-1

The Codfish Dream: Chronicles of a West Coast Fishing Guide

David Giblin

ISBN 978-1-77203-242-0

Gilly the Ghillie: More Chronicles of a West Coast Fishing Guide

David Giblin

ISBN 978-1-77203-335-9

Never Shoot a Stampede Queen: A Rookie Reporter in the Cariboo

Mark Leiren-Young

ISBN 978-1-89497-452-3

heritagehouse.ca